The Forgotten Dream of American Public Education

Robert V. Bullough, Jr.

The Forgotten Dream of American Public Education

IOWA STATE UNIVERSITY PRESS / AMES

TO MY WIFE, DAWN ANN,
AND TO OUR CHILDREN,
JOSHUA, SETH, ADAM, AND RACHEL

Robert V. Bullough, Jr. is Associate Professor of Educational Studies
at the University of Utah.

Chapter 2, "On Making Good Students," appeared originally in *The Journal of General Education,* copyright 1986, and is reprinted with the permission of the Pennsylvania State University Press. Chapter 6, "School Knowledge and Human Experience," appeared originally in *The Educational Forum,* copyright 1987, and is reprinted with the permission of Kappa Delta Pi, International Honor Society in Education.

Composed by Iowa State University Press
Printed in the United States of America

First edition, 1988

Library of Congress Cataloging-in-Publication Data

Bullough, Robert V., 1949–
    The forgotten dream of American public education.

    Bibliography: p.
    Includes index.
    1. Public schools—United States. 2. Education—Social aspects—United States. 3. Education and state—United States. I. Title.
LA217.B85   1988   371'.01'0973   88–6786
ISBN 0–8138–0008–0

CONTENTS

Preface   *vii*

1. Public Education and the Collapse
   of the Public World   *3*

2. On Making Good Students   *22*

3. Sorting and Labeling   *37*

4. Excellence and Testing   *50*

5. Teachers and the Real World of Teaching   *67*

6. School Knowledge and Human Experience   *90*

7. Creativity and Schooling   *109*

8. Schooling Metaphors   *123*

   Notes   *137*

   Index   *145*

PREFACE

AMERICANS have a rather low opinion of public schools and of the teachers who work within them. Teaching is perceived as an easy job nowhere near as demanding or as worthy as that of the physician or the lawyer. Parents think nothing of denigrating their children's teachers when they believe something is even slightly amiss, and accuse them of committing all sorts of heinous crimes against childhood without compunction. After all, anyone can be a teacher.

In contrast, few Americans would ever think of taking issue with their physician about a diagnosis and treatment that is believed to be faulty, nor would they question their lawyer's explanation of a contract just signed. These persons are seen as experts in possession of arcane knowledge and respected for it. We are impressed by their training, give homage to their degrees and pay their fees. Teachers do not so easily impress. Perhaps we Americans are too familar with teachers to be awed, having spent on average more than twelve years in school. Their weaknesses are well known. Maybe we would feel the same way toward surgeons if we had spent twelve years in operating rooms observing their failures and successes. But, we have not. We have, however, witnessed the errors of countless teachers and have occasionally been their victims. As a result, the view is commonly held that there is little skill or knowledge involved in teaching.

I hear a lot of complaints about teachers and about schools. Friends know that I have been a teacher and am now a teacher educator, so perhaps I should expect a little ear bending.

It is true, there is no denying that not all is right with American public schools or with teachers. But, what strikes me about the many discussions I have had about education, aside from how exercised everyone becomes and how enthusiastically they share tales of woe, is that so much is expected of teachers and schools, and so little of ourselves. It is so very easy to find fault because Americans want it all.

There are, however, limits to what can be delivered. Unfortunately, as a nation we apparently have not learned this lesson. In the face of a crumbling public world, we continue a century-long convenient tradition of transferring responsibility for social, economic, and political problems to the schools. *A Nation at Risk,* produced by the President's Commission on Excellence in Education, reflects this tendency by urging that our apparent inability as a nation to compete internationally is the result of school failure. Economic inequality, too, is defined essentially as an educational problem. Similarly, schools are supposed to do something about such concerns as the egregious rise in teenage pregnancy rates, the rise in drug abuse, and the spread of venereal disease. Teachers are supposed to solve all these problems and educate the young to boot.

Unfortunately, the institution of schooling was simply not designed to do all that is required of it. It was never meant to carry the full educational burden of society. For some purposes it works very well; for others, it leaves much to be desired. As an institution, the public schools took shape around the turn of the century as a reflection of our respect for and trust in American business. The factory was its ideal and efficiency, understood very narrowly, was its goal. Eggcrate classrooms, standardized curriculum and class size, bells, lines, grades, ability grouping, hierarchy, bureaucracy, and rigid job descriptions are all manifestations of having pursued this ideal. The model has proven itself suitable for domesticating large numbers of students and for judging, sorting, and certifying them. It has not, however, proven itself in other ways. It does little to encourage creativity, imagination, caring, social sensitivity, risk taking, and public world participation.

What the schools do well and what they do poorly are both sources of disappointment. Expectations are contradictory.

Schools are supposed to judge and sort talent while at the same time furthering social equality. They are supposed to encourage development of democratic attitudes and values while maintaining tight control over large numbers of potentially disruptive students. And, they are to satisfy the desire for high standardized achievement test scores while honoring diversity. The result is that we Americans love and hate our schools; we want them to change even as we want them to stay as we remember them to be.

The schools and those who serve within them try to respond to all that is asked. But, in continuing to heap upon them ever larger numbers of increasingly complex demands, while often insisting that the essential features of schooling remain unchanged, failure is a certainty. It is too seldom realized that many of the problems that are so troubling are not fundamentally reflections of either poor teachers, or administrators (though some are), but rather of the system that has been created and come to be taken for granted, and of our own inability to agree on what we expect of the public schools within a troubled public world. Clearly, the people who work within the public schools are better than the system through which they attempt to meet our expectations. It is time to begin to reconsider what we want of our teachers and schools.

In the essays that follow I explore in somewhat personal terms several of the educational issues I find most troubling and some of the possibilities that exist for reform. These issues and how I approach them reflect my belief that the fundamental purpose of public education is the cultivation of civic virtue in its many forms. While this is an old-fashioned aim, it is the only one consistent with our republican traditions. And, oddly enough, it is the only one that holds out hope for a future worthy of a democratic people.

Eight essays follow. Within the first essay, "Public Education and the Collapse of the Public World," I address the widespread loss of faith of Americans in the idea of public schooling in the light of the destruction of the public world, and raise a question that runs throughout the remaining essays: how can the public schools help re-create the public world? In the second essay, "On Making Good Students," I describe the qualities students are encouraged to develop through their experience of schooling and discuss these in relation to the qualities required for a society to be humane. In the third essay, "Sorting and Labeling," I critique the commonplace assumptions that underpin the commitment to sorting and labeling young people. In the fourth essay, "Excellence and Testing," I question the assumptions upon which standardized testing rests and challenge the tendency to define excellence by test scores. In the fifth essay, "Teachers and the Real World of Teaching," I describe what schooling is like for teachers, and what it does to them. In the sixth essay, "School Knowledge and Human Experience," I analyze the type and quality of school knowledge presented to the young, and describe promising directions for improvement. In the seventh essay, "Creativity and Schooling," I discuss the place of creativity in the public schools and the conditions necessary for its development. In the concluding essay, "Schooling Metaphors," I return to the theme of imagining public schooling differently and analyze some of the metaphors used by Americans to think about public education. I propose an alternative metaphor, school as community, as a means of thinking about public education and the public world.

I wish to thank several individuals for providing helpful feedback on the various drafts of these essays. A teacher, Judy Jardine, and her husband, Stephen, gave insightful criticism at an important time in the manuscript's development. As always, my colleague Earl Harmer proved to be a merciless critic for which I am grateful. The encouragement of Walt McPhie, Craig Kridel, Paul Klohr, and Stanley Goldstein was much appreciated as was the support of my wife, Dawn Ann, and my mother, Dolores. Most of all I want to thank my father, friend, and colleague, Robert V. Bullough, Sr., for reading and criticizing the entire manuscript. He is a much more insightful critic than he realizes.

The Forgotten Dream of American Public Education

1

Public Education and the Collapse
of the Public World

Americans are beginning to doubt the efficacy of public schooling. Costs are rising and the feeling is widespread that we are not getting our money's worth. In some parts of the country the idea of a head tax is being seriously entertained — some Americans feel resentful about having to pay for the education of other people's children. Report after report has come out adding items to the growing list of supposed failings. Many Americans are ready to jump ship and are only awaiting the opportunity. Political conservatives are willing to help taxpayers overboard by urging that Congress pass a voucher bill that would provide tax dollars to private schools. What has happened? How have so many Americans come to lose their faith in public education even as schooling seems to be increasing in importance?

Only a few generations ago schooling was not very important to most Americans. Once a young person became fairly proficient in the three R's, schooling had achieved its purposes. Times have changed, however. Gradually, young people have come to spend ever greater portions of their lives in school. Virtually every young person now completes the ninth grade, more than three out of four graduate from high school and millions go on to college. Schooling is now of immense importance.

There are several reasons for the change. Around the turn

3

of the century new occupations were formed that required school-related skills, jobs like clerking, for example. Young people who wanted such jobs began spending longer periods of time in school. Simultaneously, work for school-age young people became less plentiful as child labor became increasingly unprofitable for American business. Also, with growing prosperity many parents became better able to afford keeping their children in school past the early grades in the hope that they would enjoy more prosperous futures.

The increasing complexity of citizenship obligations has also helped make schooling more important. When Thomas Jefferson presented his Bill for the More General Diffusion of Knowledge (1779) to the Virginia assembly he thought only three years of schooling in reading, writing, cyphering, and history was adequate preparation for all children to achieve full participation in society. His colleagues saw this as a radical idea, disagreed with it, and defeated the bill.[1] Sixty years later Horace Mann thought eight years of schooling necessary for full participation in society. And now, a good case could be made that at least some college education is necessary.

An additional reason, seldom considered, is that there has been a gradual transferal of educational responsibilities from other institutions — family, church, labor organizations, and political parties — to the schools. Although many Americans complain that the schools should not be dealing with such topics as sex education, they look around and realize that there are some serious problems that are not being dealt with adequately by too many families, and so look toward the schools for assistance. There appears to be nowhere else to turn. How else can such commonplace statements as that made by Daniel Moynihan be accounted for? Like many Americans the senator is gravely concerned about the future of the American black family in which well over half of all children are born to young, unmarried women. He concludes that teachers are not doing an adequate job preventing teenage pregnancies. "Schools don't need to teach morality," he says, they "should teach common sense. Teachers must pound it into [students'] heads, into their backsides if necessary, that they cannot have children so young."[2] This statement was made straight-faced and sincerely. Though while the senator does not think schools can change this situation alone, he has a remarkable faith in the power of schooling to influence the decisions of young people. He is also deeply troubled.

Educators have had a very difficult time merely coping with, let alone adequately responding to, the problems arising from the increased numbers of students enrolled in school. In addition to these problems there are those arising from expanding responsibilities and growing expectations. The initial shock of increasing enrollments was a severe one. For example, there were only 202,000 high school students in the United States in 1890, but by 1900 there were over 500,000 and the growth rate accelerated thereafter. Even housing all these students and finding a sufficient number of adults willing and able to teach them proved difficult. Between 1890 and 1905, for instance, over five thousand new high schools were built across the country.[3]

Young people representing many and diverse backgrounds found themselves crammed into schools. With their arrival in the upper grades a battle began between the curriculum, which represented a genteel version of the adult world, and the child destined to work in the nation's teeming industries.[4] Educators split over how best to handle their new clients. Those who believed in maintaining academic standards and who cherished classical subjects found themselves opposed by self-appointed reformers who argued that schools should be relevant to the lives of young people and responsive to social problems. School had to be good for something. Each subject area had to be justified as functional; nothing was good in and of itself. In the name of democracy, young people were thrown into schools, and in the name of democracy the curriculum was fragmented into innumerable slices of content, each reflecting a very different view of what was of most educational worth. Tracks were formed reflecting probable destinies: classical for college-bound students, scientific for the more technically oriented, vocational for those headed into the trades, and general for everyone else.

This was not all that was done in the name of relevance, of making the schools serve the needs of society and of students. *Needs* is a key word here. Throughout much of this century need has been a word of considerable consequence to educators.

It has been used to justify every imaginable educational innova-
tion, silly and substantial. But what is typically missing in discussions of need is the realization that some kind of standard
must be employed to determine what a legitimate need is and
whether or not it has a reasonable claim on institutional resources. Without such an articulated standard, it is difficult to
establish grounds for denial. In effect, educators, in their enthusiasm for the cause of public education and their faith in the
reforming power of schooling, opened the door to almost all
claims of need.

This suited our society well. As the first and only nation
built explicitly upon an educational foundation, democracy and
education have long been inextricably linked in the American
mind. To Americans even political and economic problems have
been seen as educational problems—we have been loath to admit that there might be something fundamentally wrong with
either our economic or political systems. It has been comforting,
even commonplace, to understand social problems as originat-
ing in individual moral failings. And it has been the task of
education to overcome such failing.

Schools were supposed to do it all: provide showers for
filthy kids, food, courses in personal hygiene, morals, bricklaying, and later, drivers' education, careers, sex education (now
to include instruction in so-called safe sex), and several levels of
math, English, history, and science. And, they were, and still
are, expected to ameliorate economic and political problems:
provide a means for economic mobility, soften social class differences, defend the free enterprise system, civilize the uncivil—
especially the foreign-born—prevent crime, instill good work
habits, and teach patriotism.

Disappointment was certain to follow. We have run head-
on into the limitations of the public school to provide for all our
expectations. Yet, Americans continue to expect more, and our
frustration grows.

The voucher bill introduced not long ago in Congress plays
on this frustration by suggesting that it would actually be good
for the public schools if the federal government makes it easier
for parents to place their children in private schools. The bill
would provide six hundred dollars to parents of children who

need remedial schooling to enable them to attend the school of their choice. The door would then be opened, however slightly, to public funding of private schooling. Supposedly, public education will benefit by this move. One advocate, secretary of education, William Bennett, for example, believes the bill, if enacted, "would promote a healthy rivalry among schools . . . and would allow parents to choose the program that best meets the needs of their children."[5] Orrin Hatch, the Senate sponsor, enthusiastically agrees that the "plan will foster worthwhile competition and give an incentive to schools to improve their programs."[6]

Discussion of reforming American schooling through competition is common now. Creating marketplace conditions in which individual schools compete with one another for students is widely hailed as the means to radical improvement. Myron Lieberman, for one, argues that "the private sector delivers other so-called public services more cheaply, and often better, than public agencies. I see no reason that it cannot do the same with education."[7] Competition is not the only element of the marketplace that is now being seen as worthy of emulation. The way in which resources are organized is also viewed as desirable. For instance, Chester Finn, assistant secretary of education, believes that principals should function like corporate executives, rather than as principal-teachers. "A principal should be more an executive than a teacher and more an executive than a civil servant."[8]

On the face of it, providing access to those unable to afford private remedial education seems like a wonderful idea, and upon first glance, the idea of having free choice and competition among schools strikes a resonant chord. But, a closer look gives reason to pause and wonder. Reforming the schools around marketplace values means abandoning the citizenship ideal that originally gave purpose and direction to public education, an ideal that served as a standard by which to make educational decisions. This would be a profound loss.

The primary purpose of Jefferson's Bill for the More General Diffusion of Knowledge was to promote democratic citizenship. He believed there was an intimate link between democracy and education. His concern was simple. In order for all citizens to participate fully in the public world, education should be available to everyone, at no cost. Moreover, he thought all young people of all backgrounds should be educated together, for in no other way could they come to recognize and understand their common interests. Such an understanding was essential to obtaining wide participation within the public world, which, in turn, was the key element to making certain that America would continue to reflect the conditions necessary for full human development. "It is an axiom of my mind," he wrote to George Washington, "that our liberty can never be safe but in the hands of the people themselves."[9] But, the people must possess the knowledge and skill necessary for the task, which requires that they be provided "a certain degree of instruction." As mentioned, he thought three years of education in reading, writing, arithmetic and the study of history sufficient. Literacy and a free press were means for understanding the responsibilities of citizenship, which included keeping tabs on the use of power. History was the study of great ideas and great lives that were inspiring exemplars of civic virtue.

Jefferson had a second purpose: he wanted to make certain America would have the benefits of an educated and civically minded elite to guide the state in ways consistent with natural law, the source of "certain inalienable rights." In order to police the elite, citizens had to understand the issues and be able to make reasonable decisions about them. Only in this way could they preserve their liberty. Jefferson thought by bringing together all young people, regardless of background, and treating them to an identical three-year education, and then allowing the most able to move on to additional education, the public schools would eventually help a "natural aristocracy" form. This group would replace the false aristocracy that had, because of inheritance, improperly assumed positions of leadership. Leaders would arise out of and always be responsible to the mass of people.[10]

In coming to his understanding of public education, Jefferson assumed that schools would exist within a public world that itself was educational. Schools were not to bear the full burden of educating citizens. He assumed a public world to which individuals had access, one that was morally and socially superior to that of any other society. The very possibility of their participation within this world as equals confirmed, to his mind, America's superiority over the old world. A similar assumption was held by Horace Mann and other early champions of public education. This understanding was based upon fragments of a classical worldview in which the public world was a place where men met as equals to work together to achieve perfection. Politics and citizenship were educational activities, good in and of themselves. Men came together within the public sphere to participate in and extend a shared vision of the good. And, for this good, they voluntarily accepted limitations on their freedom.[11] Although we rightfully fault the classical view for excluding women from participation in the public world and for embracing slavery, the ideal itself is a worthy one, and it stands in harsh contrast to the view conveyed by Senator Hatch and Secretary Bennett.

Consider the view of citizenship implicit in the voucher bill and in the arguments presented in its favor. Quietly hiding under the surface of this apparently magnanimous gesture is a set of troubling assumptions about the public world. I wonder what it means if Senator Hatch is correct, that the essence of democracy is the right of the individual to choose among competing educational products in the same sense as selecting among brands of soup? I further wonder if competition is the key to the improvement of schooling as is now so widely believed, even by many of the nation's governors?[12] At its extreme, such a view reflects an emaciated and hollow conception of citizenship, presenting the public world as nothing more than an arena within which competing and self-centered individuals — "arbitrary centers of volition" — exercise their freedom independently and without consideration of the interests of others.[13] From this viewpoint, schooling is like any other service, and whatever anyone wants should be provided at public expense. The obligation of the school, therefore, is only to satisfy the individual; what is good for the individual is good for all. The implication is that no common good exists; serving the interests of the individual, however narrowly construed, is all that matters.

The current antipathy toward public schooling is partly an unfortunate and unexpected outcome of the Herculean efforts of countless thousands of educators who willingly responded to the pressure for schools to take on ever greater responsibilities. In the process of doing so, they helped elevate the importance of schooling, simultaneously and unwittingly making it unlikely that it could ever fulfill those responsibilities. For this educators cannot be faulted. They took on more responsibilities, not out of ambition, but out of a genuine desire to help young people. What they could not have possibly known was that in doing so they actually contributed to the conditions that led to the increase in expectations in the first place. They helped other institutions shed their educational responsibilities until schooling became synonymous with education and the public world lost much of its educational power.

THE FAILURE OF CIVIC VIRTUE
AND THE PROMOTION OF UTILITY

With the crumbling of the public world, the foundation of public education itself has been severely shaken. The cornerstone of the foundation is the aim of citizenship without which there are few if any fundamental differences between private and public education, save the ability of private schools to deny services. Public schooling has lost its center; it is everything and nothing even as its apparent social and symbolic significance is increasing. It is not at all surprising that questions are being raised about the viability of the public school. There is no end to human demand, and no possible way for a single institution to satisfy that demand.

Having lost citizenship as an ideal, the defense of public education rests upon its utility in satisfying individual wants, or, at its base level, the purpose of all schooling, public and private, is to get a job. The belief that schooling must be directly relevant to a vocation makes a high degree of dissatisfaction inevitable, and leaves little with which to defend public schooling against its detractors. Such a defense is a justification of schooling, certainly not of *public* schooling. Nevertheless, the argument deserves consideration because it has been a prime motivator behind calls for public school reform. It is the vocational need to reform presented by The President's Commission on Excellence in Education in *A Nation At Risk* that is most remembered. Because Americans are moving into an information age, the "demand for highly skilled workers in new fields is accelerating rapidly," the commission asserts, and the demand must be met. Everyone must be prepared for highly technical jobs for the security of young people themselves and that of the nation. To this end, the entire curriculum is being reorganized; the purpose of education is to gain one of these jobs.

But, is this assertion true? Must all young people be educated to assume high-tech jobs? And more to the point, is this solid ground upon which to base an argument for continued support of public education? Are we in for more disappointment? It certainly is true that among the fastest growing occupations are computer system analysis, data processing, and computer operation; these are highly skilled jobs, no doubt. But, it is also true that the total number of jobs expected to be created in these areas is comparatively small. In fact, there is not a single high-tech job among the twenty occupations expected to produce the most openings between now and the turn of the century. The five occupations that will lead the way — janitors, nurses' aids, sales clerks, cashiers, and waiters and waitresses — require little training at all.[14] If the purpose of public education is to land a fancy job then almost all young people are heading for disappointment. Given current economic trends, why should young Americans, whose future leads under the Golden Arches to Ronald McDonald's, believe us when we tell them that education is important? A little math, a bit of spelling, good work habits, and a pleasant personality will do nicely for work of this kind, and they know it, to the dismay of teachers.

The answer is depressing. They should believe us because there is cash value in schooling, represented by the diploma. A diploma is necessary to get a job even at McDonald's, not the study of history, English or mathematics. The diploma signals to employers that a young person has learned how to behave and to work hard. But, even this is now being questioned. For example, the Committee for Economic Development, a public research group composed of 225 trustees who are mostly top corporate executives, reached the conclusion after a three-year study that "an alarming number" of students leave school thinking the adult world will put up with tardiness, absenteeism, and misbehavior. The report stated that "if schools tolerate excessive absenteeism, truancy, tardiness, or misbehavior, we cannot expect students to meet standards of minimum performance or behavior either in school or as adults."[15] Employers want assurance that possession of a diploma indicates that a young person will be a good worker.

There is, however, some good news. Through public education anyone and everyone can obtain a diploma who remains long enough (this certainly is not so with private schooling). Recognizing the cash value of the diploma has led educators to work mightily to make certain all students graduate. To this end, programs of various kinds are provided to take care of those who stumble along the way. Such programs frequently reflect different, sometimes lower, academic standards. When the aim of schooling is to gain a credential, the existence of lower standards may be easily ignored. Happily, however, the Justice Department, among others, is unwilling to ignore them. In late 1985, for example, an investigation was launched into charges that minority students were being placed in programs "that were not teaching them the basic fundamentals but were geared to just getting them through and giving them a diploma."[16]

Upon reflection this is offensive. But why? Whose values does it offend? The belief of Americans that the central purpose of education is to get ahead is paralleled by the belief that the competition ought to be fair, or at least have the appearance of fairness. Echoing Jefferson, merit ought to be what counts, even when frequently it is not. By combining the belief that the primary function of schooling is to prepare young people for the world of work with an additional assumption that school success ought to be used to distribute rewards—which requires firm performance standards—we come as close as is possible to making a unique cash value argument for public schooling. But, it also fizzles and falls flat. In this view, life is a contest and every one has the right to compete individually; the strong will rise to the top where, because of having proven themselves meritorious, they will be handsomely rewarded. This is the essence of the American understanding of justice.[17]

In the battle for position, public schools have an important part to play. Their function, unlike the private schools, is to enroll everyone (except, of course, those who can buy their way out), identify the talented, sort them, treat them in special ways through formal and informal tracking, and move them along to higher education where winnowing will continue. They also gently help young people who cannot succeed to realize their limitations and accept them; they justify and legitimate failure. Someone, after all, must fall by the wayside because there is not enough room at the top for everyone. So it is the task of the school alone to "[keep] us from one another's throats."[18] Within this theory then, the essence of public education is to put everyone together to compete as individuals for limited opportunities. Because, at least in principle, all young people have the same opportunity to prove their worth under similar conditions in school, failure is a personal matter. Ultimately, those who get ahead will deserve success, those who fail at least had the opportunity to try. For trying, we will give most of them a diploma, which is what they wanted anyway.

The argument cannot bear scrutiny. The difficulty is not only that the public schools have not done a fully adequate job identifying and educating the talented and that private schools sometimes do better, nor that it is unreasonable to expect the parents of children who fail to pay for the continuing education of those who succeed. Rather, the central difficulty resides in the idea that success is the result of individual striving and merit alone.[19] No one competes solely as an individual. Each person competes as a historical and genetic repository of traits, and experiences that have developed those traits in particular ways. These are factors over which the individual has little control. For good or ill we compete as representatives of the contexts within which we were reared. It is certainly true that schooling can influence individual development. But it is also generally true that both the public and the private schools, as currently organized, confirm rather than soften the social class differences among us, even while striving to obtain behavior consistent with running orderly institutions. They do this by sorting and labeling young people, simultaneously distributing knowledge unequally. The race for knowledge and position is far from fair even at the starting line; most of those who get ahead even within a public school setting begin with tremendous advantages.

This is a depressing generalization to those Americans nourished on the belief that they alone earned their rewards. So pleased are they with their success, that they even think themselves more virtuous than those who fell behind. Merit has been confused with virtue. Minority high school graduates have learned this lesson the hard way. High unemployment rates among minorities cannot be explained by a lack of credentials or even of ability. For those whose families are relatively well off, schooling, especially private schooling, is a means for preventing position slippage.

The conclusion is forced upon us that if Americans continue to insist that the central reason for education is to prepare young people for the world of work, whether it be in the professions or McDonald's, then there is little reason to continue in the persistent, but sickly, stance against separate kinds of schools, private or public, for different kinds of children. Why not stop fighting destiny. Americans should wholeheartedly embrace class education, as England does, rather than continue to schizophrenically maintain a system that is unable to adequately prepare an elite or a trained workforce, and is therefore unsatisfying. Why not give tax dollars to private schools that may be able to meet these aims? And, why not uncompromisingly use test scores to separate the intellectually able from the less able early, and help both groups to accept the inevitable? Afterall, everyone knows that children have different futures, so why not make certain they get to them quickly without wasting precious educational resources and effort?!

We have come a full circle; without the promotion of democratic citizenship as a central aim, public education loses its reason for being. Americans have lost a vision of the public world as separate from the world of work: "The citizen has been swallowed up by the 'economic man.'"[20] Yet, vocational arguments for public schooling are sadly unconvincing even as they continue to be the arguments presented to young people and their parents. At the same time, the public schools persist in operating in ways that make it increasingly difficult to make other arguments convincingly. Young people of different backgrounds still march through the school's doors, but once there they have very different experiences of schooling. As they progress from grade to grade they share fewer and fewer classes together, and even when they do, they are treated very differently. Hostility, frustration, disappointment, and resignation follow.

Our schools are helping to establish and justify a three-tiered occupational structure while trying to maintain a commitment to social equality. At the top of the pyramid are a few highly skilled members of a decision-making elite who enjoy exceptional opportunities. They serve a small group of Americans who own the vast majority of the nation's wealth and are handsomely rewarded for it.[21] Based on the narrowness of their field of expertise and their positions, they define what are the essential problems and their solutions. Frequently they have little faith in the American people, and even scorn them, as exemplified by recent insider trading scandals on Wall Street.

The next level of the pyramid is occupied by skilled professionals whose main purpose is to carry out the programs of the elite. This group has little concern for the ethical implications of these programs. Their goal is to fulfill their responsibilities. For both groups " 'being good' " is a "matter of having the right answers."[22]

Finally, the bottom of the pyrmaid is composed of a large pool of unskilled, unorganized, and politically vulnerable workers who have little job security, are highly mobile, and poorly paid. They possess the vote, but find little reason to exercise it.

Within society now the gaps between these groups are already widening, and when put in these terms, many who think public education's primary task ought to be to prepare young people for work begin to squirm. A huge pool of comparatively uneducated citizens who possess the vote is potentially dangerous. Lingering in many Americans is a belief that, although getting a job is the most important aim of education, it ought to include something more. Perhaps it is for this reason that Americans have not as yet fully embraced vouchers as a means for school reform.[23] Nevertheless, we are torn. Americans are really not very enthusiastic about class education, but as parents we do want out own children to get ahead whatever the cost: principles and other people's children be damned. Such priorities are understandable but troubling.

The word *public* has increasingly come to connote spreading around the cost of benefits received by an elite few. There are many examples of this, not the least of which is the heavy public subsidy given to legal and medical education to produce attorneys and physicians whose services a great many Americans cannot afford. Nevertheless, the belief is widespread that the future is dependent upon developing an intellectual and technical elite who are supposedly capable of understanding and solving the complex problems facing America. Few alternatives seem reasonable. As parents, we want our children to enjoy membership in this group and we want the group to be given special educational treatment. Implicitly, given the complexity of twentieth-century America, many Americans may have simply given up on the idea that most everyone is capable of understanding issues and of making informed decisions, although many wish it were not so. Public education is supported because it is a ritual; it helps keep young people off of the streets and, echoing Horace Mann, it helps civilize them. Education is not the primary aim of schooling. Rather, it is the socialization and control of other peoples' children. For our own children we parents want something better and many of us would gladly abandon the public school to achieve it if necessary. We want our children to get to the top. When this hope fails, resentment and anger follow producing enemies of the public schools.

A NEW AWARENESS AND A NEW RESPONSIBILITY
TO THE PUBLIC WORLD

The public school has not been alone in denigrating the public world. Indeed, it too has been a victim, particularly of an economy that has systematically deskilled and fragmented labor.[24] Work, for most Americans, is becoming increasingly unchallenging and uninteresting. Personality and initiative find few outlets within the workplace. Nor is room found for perhaps our most cherished values, independence and individualism, which find expression elsewhere. Playing on these values and twisting them, the mass media, servant of advanced capitalism, has been convincing; through conspicuous consumption we express who and what we are. The lessons of "Dallas" and "Dynasty" have not been lost on America, even while we vaguely sense our consumption only produces an "anxious conformity."[25] Lincoln Continentals, Porsches, and fancy clothes let the world know who and what we are. Males and females consume one another like other goods and services. It is little wonder that alongside "Dallas" and "Dynasty" are children's shows, such as the Saturday morning "Punky Brewster" cartoon, that portray adults as shortsighted, dimwitted, and foolish large children.

Disengagement from the public world has also been encouraged by the centralization of decision making in the hands of a few experts who rotate through corporation boardrooms and government offices. Now, to be politically involved is to vote, and few citizens even do that. Rather, escape is sought from "the problems of the public world," which are left to experts of various kinds.[26] As citizenship responsibilities have dwindled, elections have become managed media events in which few attempts are made to explain the issues. The candidate who makes the attempt is apt to be viewed as distant and uncharismatic, too intellectual. It is now character that matters, as former presidential candidate Gary Hart and uncounted other fallen angels have discovered. Issues are lost in powdered smiling faces and rhetoric; to vote is to choose between slick professionally packaged products designed in response to pollster surveys of tastes and desires. Politicians are professionals intent on staying in office and who, as a result, are fearful to offend and are willing, even eager, to sell the future to the present while most Americans stand idly by, disconnected spectators of what was the public world.

We are facing a critical moment in our history. There is a continuing trend toward further debilitation of the public world and of public education in a celebration of a bankrupt conception of individualism. Personally, I struggle with the question of whether or not it is possible for the public schools to help re-create the public world. I think so, but clearly it is foolhardy to expect them to lead the way. Fortunately, there are signs that the schools will not have to face the task alone. The vitality and increased popularity of public television and the rise in popularity of programs like "The Cosby Show," indicate that some members of the media are beginning to take the importance of teaching values that enhance rather than denigrate the public world more seriously. That such programs are extremely popular also suggests that the American people sense that something is missing—there is an unsatisfied hunger that the ability to consume cannot satisfy. This hunger is evident in the emergence of such organizations as the Campaign for Economic Democracy and the Institute for the Study of Civic Values in Philadelphia, which aim at re-creating a shared sense of civic virtue.[27] A few religious groups are also becoming positively involved as well.

College and university faculties are also waking up to their civic responsibilities. For some time there has been concern expressed about the quality of the students being sent for higher education by the public schools. The problem is not only that the students have some skill deficiencies, but also that they rarely possess essential character traits. To address weaknesses in skills, universities have increased their admission standards. Now, they must take a bolder step and begin to consider ways of helping the young develop the intellectual and ethical qualities essential to establishing a vital public world, a world characterized by commitment to the quest for consensus about the common good. Colleges and universities, where narrow vocationalism reigns supreme, must take a very hard look at the values they are helping to instill in the young. Efforts of organizations like Campus Compact, which involves 120 college presidents and chancellors who are committed to "devise ways of strengthening students' commitment to public service," are promising.[28]

To identify common interests and then to elevate them over special interests and to build commitment to a shared vision of the future is far from an easy matter. Part of the task for education is to create a consensus around skills, attitudes, and under-standing essential for full participation within the public world. Some of these are fairly easy to identity and accept. The ability to read, write, think mathematically, and analyze problems and evidence is necessary. It is also necessary to have an understand-ing of our history and of how our society is interdependent with others. Moreover, it is the right of all people, including those who end up working at McDonald's, to have access to the means used by experts to define our world. They must have the knowl-edge necessary to penetrate the obscurantism that masquerades as expertise.

There are also attitudes and values derived from our often-times forgotten democractic traditions that require nurturing. These are much more difficult to identify and more controver-sial, but nonetheless fundamental. Social sensitivity, the ability to stand in the other person's shoes, is one such attitude. Another is the willingness to suspend judgement, to tolerate, even honor, differences and to compromise. A third is the ability to live with ambiguity and to accept uncertainty. And, still another is the courage and the willingness to take risks in de-fense of principles. None of these skills or attitudes develop naturally. Our schools and colleges must provide young people with experiences that will foster their development.

There is another body of qualities essential to a vital public world that is only now being acknowledged seriously. As noted, the classical public world was a male-dominated world. Oddly, the values traditionally associated with masculinity that, not su-prisingly, have found their way into our economic and political systems in which domination, control, and aggression are high values, may actually have contributed to the collapse of the public world. In effect, these values need to be softened, feminized. If we are to re-create the public world, and if it is to be an ideal world, then compassion, nurturing, service, sacri-fice, receptivity, patience, caring, commitment, and relatedness must be cherished. The experience young people have of school ought to help them develop these qualities, without which, edu-cation, in any fundamental sense, is impossible.

The peculiar and particular responsibility of public school-ing is civic education. Its purpose, in the words of R. Freeman

Butts, is to "serve the general welfare of a democratic society" and to "achieve a sense of community."[29] It is not to sort young people; it is to help all of them master the tools and develop the attitudes necessary for full participation in our society. To do this job adequately requires all the school time available and more.

Responsibilities now assumed by the schools must be trimmed and the first one that should go is specific vocational education. Public schooling is only indirectly of vocational worth. As an aim, vocation belongs to other institutions, most notably technical and professional schools, and business. For this reason varsity athletics, for example, just like bricklaying, health careers, and TV repair, belongs outside of the public school curriculum, as do advanced courses in the disciplines that properly belong on the college campuses. Drivers' education and many of the other service courses offered by the schools should also be abandoned.

If citizenship is to be the primary concern of public schooling, then careful attention must be given to the methods of teaching and to the context of teaching. For example, history and science can be taught vocationally when the goal is to make "little historians" or "little scientists." The context of teaching either enhances or inhibits the identification of shared interests and the building of community. At a minimum, young people of diverse backgrounds need to share a significant portion of their day learning together about one another and about the society and world within which they live, which is now rarely the case. Education must become increasingly centered on how the world is experienced and made meaningful. Americans need to recognize and build on the elements of our shared normative framework, our republican and biblical traditions, that now seem so strained. To do this requires a de-emphasis on judging and sorting the young, on competition, and an increased emphasis on developing cooperation, commitment, and caring. Indeed, schooling ought to be the practice of civic virtue. Schools must, therefore, be smaller, less threatening organizations in which teachers and young people enjoy a high degree of responsibility and ownership. Moreover, the school must become a community unto itself as it reaches out into the larger social world to study and challenge it.

The deflation of the public world has been gradual, so rejuvenation and recreation will also be slow. Public education has an important role to play that may be no less significant than fundamental economic restructuring. On the educational front rejuvenation will require a leap of faith. The essence of this faith is that we are deeply and fundamentally united by the human condition, and that we share common interests and aspirations that can only come to fruition within a genuine community. Moreover, it is an article of faith that common people have the capacity to make reasonable decisions, that they can understand the issues before us with eyes and hearts open to see and to feel the consequences of their actions on those distant in space and time. And, it is part of the faith that individuals only find full expression in and through others; individual development is dependent upon the development of others. This faith beckons to future generations who deserve better than to inherit a crippling national debt just as it speaks to those for whom talk about justice and equality is more bitter than sweet.

In the essays that follow, I address a few of the ways in which the public schools are contributing to the vitiation of the public world and suggest some possibilities for reformation. My hope is to encourage you, the reader, to think of public schooling differently; to begin questioning the taken for granted in ways that might lead to a reconsideration of the role schools, as well as colleges and universities, might play in revitalizing the public world, and then to get personally involved.

2

On Making Good Students

E VERY spring I attend a scholarship committee meeting. Our task is to sift through scholarship applications of four or five dozen high school seniors. The task is an especially difficult one; these are not just ordinary students, they are exceptional in every respect. Because there are far more applicants than scholarships, we must make distinctions among them. Small differences, unimportant in virtually every other context, loom large: membership in clubs, involvement in student government, participation in volunteer work as well as grade point average and types of courses taken, all count. The students apparently understand this and prepare in advance for what is to come. When they begin preparing, I do not know. I do know, however, that by the time the finalists arrive for their interviews with the committee they are ready.

Proof of preparation comes in many forms. As the students enter the room where their interview is to take place, a few distribute professionally prepared vitas. I continue to be amazed, when reading these documents, how anyone so young could have found time to do so much. Work experience and academic, athletic, artistic, and citizenship awards are all boldly noted on their vitas, and time spent engaged in good works is prominently displayed by some. All are smartly dressed. A

An early version of this essay first appeared in *The Journal of General Education*, vol. 39, no. 2 (1986).

quick review of their academic records reveals that early in their school careers they carefully mapped out where they were going. As very young people, they entered preferred programs and got the grades; very few "B" grades appear and never a "C." For the most part they answer our questions promptly and with confidence. These young people know that they are good students.

For the past few years, when I have served on this committee, it has become progressively more difficult for me to tell these young people apart. I find it nearly impossible to make distinctions among them and find no pleasure in doing so. They are all good students, perhaps too good, and it is this realization that troubles me.

The students seem alike because, for the most part, they are alike — at least on the surface. They have made their future plans and prepared their cases for us based upon an identical and shared set of assumptions about what it is to be a good student, and this is taken as necessary not only for admission into a decent college but also for obtaining scholarships. These are sophisticated, professional students who apparently learned at a very young age, and learned well, what it takes to get ahead. A single incident well illustrates the point. During a brief interlude following the completion of several student interviews, I began describing to the committee what the next person would say, have accomplished, and look like. To be silly, I embellished my description by asserting confidently that, besides having done everything and been everywhere, she would most certainly have dimples. When McKenzie (a fictious name) entered the room, vita in hand, even I was surprised to look up and see the person I had described. Greeting us, she smiled, and our surprise turned to muffled laughter; McKenzie had two perfectly placed dimples punctuating a lovely rosey complexion. More to the point, a quick glance at her vita proved that she had indeed taken all the right courses and been a member of all the right clubs. She sat down. We introduced ourselves and proceeded into the interview questions. The interview went very well; McKenzie was a *very* good student.

I am not alone in my concern. Of late, increasing attention is being given to the kind of persons our institutions are molding. We are beginning to wonder what we mean by "good student" and whether or not good students are what we need to ensure our nation's future in an increasingly competitive, complex and unfriendly political and economic world. *Higher Education and the American Resurgence*, issued in 1985 by the Carnegie Foundation for the Advancement of Teaching, for example, forcefully raises these questions. Too frequently, this study asserts, students "take safe courses, are discouraged from risky or interdisciplinary research projects, and are discouraged from challenging the ideas presented to them."[1]

Those who might take risks are prevented from doing so by "fear of censure, or distrust, or fear of failure; a stifling atmosphere; attempts to closely control behavior and thinking; restricted communication; the assumption, in the classroom and in texts that there is one right answer to every problem; and a passive role." Moreover, the education we offer to the young confirms the current trend toward narrow self-interest. Recent surveys "show a 15-year decline in expectation of participation in the political life of the country, in any form of altruism, or of concern for the interests of others. Over the same time, there has been a steady rise in student interest in those values associated with money, status, and power."[2]

Unfortunately, whereas in the past the college experience tended to help students overcome narrow parochialism, it appears at present the values of senior students mirror those of freshmen. "Only about 31 per cent of the freshman [sic] men and 27 per cent of the women expressed a strong desire to influence political structures and decisions, which improved slightly for senior men (31 per cent) and surprisingly actually declined for senior women (24 per cent)."[3] Self-interest and vocationalism have come to dominate campus life.

The good student is passive, accepting of authority, neat, clean, predictable, steady, fearful of failure, goal oriented, and, sadly, disconnected from the public world and dominated, like bad students, by narrow self-interest and vocationalism. The poor student is disruptive, difficult to manage, sloppy in work and dress, unpredictable, undependable, incapable of delaying gratification, and little concerned about the future.

Young people are not naturally good students. They must be taught. The lessons they must learn are often hard and unpleasant. It is a long, complex, and oftentimes heartbreaking process that eventually produces a McKenzie. In thousands of small ways the child-student is encouraged to leave behind the values of everyday living to embrace those of the school. This is a process of gradual socialization, involving constant surveillance of behavior, assessment of attitudes, and the dispensing of countless numbers of rewards and punishments to make certain the desired characteristics are eventually developed.

When a child enters school from a home that has encouraged values consistent with those of the school, the transition into the role of student is a comparatively easy one; when differences are pronounced, difficulties are certain to follow. When the fit is an uncomfortable one, and child and parent resistant to change, the institution responds by declaring the offender aberrant, whereupon he or she is marked and, if there is a sufficiently large number of such children, placed into a special program designed specifically to correct the weaknesses of a certain category of misfits. This action is undertaken under the guise of serving the student's needs which are understood as deficiencies.

That so many young people become good students is a tribute to the flexibility of youth and, especially, to the power of our institutions to mold and shape personalities. Like other forms of deity, institutions do their best to create people in their own image — for good and ill. Schools are no different. We only need to review our own school experience briefly to recollect instances in which the weight of the institution was brought to bear to ensure conformity to good student ideals. I think, for instance, of an interaction I had with my sixth-grade teacher who, I am certain, was little different from thousands of other teachers who currently face the nearly impossible task of managing thirty students in small, unpleasant classrooms across the nation.

Mr. Wheatley (again, a fictious name) gave his students the opportunity to paint a picture of any kind we wished. I enthusiastically painted a colorful landscape, complete with a robust scarlet cloud. I liked the painting, a lot. In anticipation of my teacher's praise, I turned my work in, only to have it soundly criticized because "clouds are not red." I was crushed. Years later, when pollution had altered the sky, I saw a cloud very much like the one I had painted and felt vindicated. Sadly, for vindication I needed to see a *real* red cloud. By then I had already learned my lesson. There is a right and wrong answer to everything, including art, and red clouds were wrong. When I had to paint clouds in the future, good student that I was, they somehow always came out white and fluffy. A second lesson learned was that to see the world differently would only bring heartache. Other stories quickly come to mind but their outcome was, for me, everywhere and almost always the same.

To understand how schools turn young people into good students we need to carefully consider what young people are allowed to do while in school and what they learn from the doing. But before we do so, a cautionary word is in order. There is no question that young people must become students; otherwise, education of any sort is impossible. As students they must come to learn a wide variety of things: to live and work with and care for others, to develop self-discipline, to master the tool skills — reading, writing, and computation — to think, and much more. These are worthy goals but unfortunately the system established to meet them is incongruous. It appears as though the student ideal that young people are encouraged to embrace (which a good many of them reject at great personal cost), in large measure, actually works against the achievement of our higher educational aspirations. The kinds of students young people are allowed to become determines the outcome of schooling. Will young people become critically minded, literate and ethically responsible citizens or something else — well socialized, but greedy, parochial, and unprincipled consumers of resources? Either outcome is possible.

The classroom door has been thrown open by John Goodlad and his colleagues who participated in "A Study of Schooling." Through their observations of 129 elementary, 362 junior high and 525 senior high classes we gain a reasonably good idea of what young people do while in school.[4] The conclusions of this study deserve our attention. Students make few, if any, decisions about their learning even though sometimes they feel that they do. Elementary classrooms are "almost entirely teacher dominated with respect to seating, grouping, content, materials, use of space, time utilization, and learning activities."[5] It is little different in the upper grades in which one might expect a greater student involvement in learning. Ninety percent of the junior high and 80 percent of the high school classes excluded students from decision making. Those few classes in which students enjoyed a measure of control over their learning tended to be in nonacademic areas such as art, physical education and vocational education, and even then, the decisions allowed tended to be "somewhat removed from the learning activity itself."[6]

Students seldom talk in classrooms and are, as a group, generally out-talked by teachers three to one. In a typical classroom 75 percent of the time is spent on instruction and 70 percent of this time is talk of some kind, usually teacher talk. While teachers talk, good students quietly listen, poor students disrupt, and very bad students are excluded from the privilege of listening.

Teaching is telling. The proof of good teaching is high standardized test scores. Of all instructional time, very little, barely 5 percent, aims at creating "the anticipation of needing to respond in students." Not even 10 percent of instructional time requires students to express an opinion, or involves them in reasoning. Apparently students are not supposed to think—that is the implicit message communicated to them. When teachers solicit student involvement, it is more often than not to answer fill-in-the-blank type questions. These convey the impression that becoming educated is to engage in a very long and extensive game of trivia: what is the capital of Wyoming? who was the sixteenth president of the United States? what is Osmosis? Another prominent use of questions is to discipline a child who appears to be wandering and put them back on task.

Because there is so little student talk in classrooms, especially those orderly classrooms that so please the casual observer, it is hardly surprising that teachers rarely respond to students. There are few opportunities to do so, unless, of course, a classroom is filled with bad students intent on disruption. For many teachers, the sign of a good lecture is that there are no student questions following its completion; if there are not any questions, then there must not be any confusion. When teachers do respond to students, unless it is for disciplinary reasons, they do so in nonpersonal ways, as though responding to one student is precisely the same as responding to another. "Good" and "all right" typically carry the burden of letting the student know that their performance is acceptable.

One outcome of holding to the view that teaching is telling, and the essence of being a good student is the ability to listen well, is that classrooms are for the most part devoid of shared laughter, enthusiasm, or even of anger honestly expressed.[7] Classrooms appear emotionally flat, but the flatness of the classroom stands in stark contrast to what transpires at recess in the elementary grades or in the hallways between class periods in the upper grades. During these times, and following the sounding of the bell that signals the end of the day, the energy of youth gushes out in many ways that adults find shocking: locker doors are slammed, friends are punched, grabbed and kicked, enemies are attacked, and boy and girl friends hugged and kissed. There is a tremendous amount of life displayed in those few moments outside of the confines of the classroom, life that begs expression and struggles for appropriate forms. The adult who has the misfortune of being near a doorway or standing in a hallway when school ends learns quickly how frightening the expression of this energy can be to those who do not possess it.

Being talked at constantly, and reminded of the importance of paying attention, are not the only classroom experiences that help form young people into students. They also spend a large portion of their days working alone on individual assignments or projects while the teacher circulates, monitoring behavior and performance. Although this pattern is most typical of the upper grades, it is also apparent in elementary school classrooms where the worksheet is king. Each of us who has attended public schools is well aware of worksheets—those single sheets of paper that contain seemingly endless lists of questions to be answered and problems to be solved. Much of the time we thought that worksheets were busy work, but completed them nevertheless. The good student does not complain about having to do worksheets, at least not vocally; rather, he or she is quietly diligent and, if a very good student, completes the work without the teacher's assistance, which means there is even less interaction. To fail to complete one's work is to invite censure.

Young people who have not yet become good students receive special help. Discipline helps the student internalize the necessity of developing the desired attitudes and behaviors. So important is the need to obtain good student behavior in the classroom that it sometimes overshadows other educational aims: good behavior becomes an aim in and of itself rather than a means to achieving other ends. Students learn this quickly and sometimes come to value appearances more than reality. They learn, for instance, to appear attentive, which pleases teachers who assume the appearance of attention to be genuine attention. Tests and occasional direct questions reveal that the shadow has been mistaken for the substance. Nevertheless, even authentic good students realize there is much to be gained by mastering appearances. Classroom life is made infinitely more bearable in this manner and no one is obviously hurt.

When we think of the meaning of "good student" few of us would knowingly associate this term with passivity, fear of failure, and all the rest. Teachers certainly would not have it this way. Many teachers, in fact, spend a considerable amount of energy trying to encourage the development of other, contrary, values. Yet, in spite of the efforts of such teachers, we continue to turn out good students in the pejorative sense, nurtured in schools in which the aim of education appears to be making young people accept and become comfortable with a multitude of unexamined and taken-for-granted constraints on their development.

If teachers know better, which many certainly do, then why do they persist in encouraging attitudes and values that are miseducative? The only reasonable conclusion, assuming teachers to be well meaning and decent people, is that the institutional and cultural context within which they work encourages development of students of this kind, while simultaneously discouraging, although not completely preventing, realization of other aims. To get a handle on the problem it is necessary to consider schooling more generally than we have thus far. Classrooms and the work of teachers must be situated in the larger context of schooling in America. There are powerful forces that encourage teachers to teach in ways that develop passivity, dependence, and self-centeredness in young people, just as there are powerful influences encouraging students to comply.

Schooling in America has served a variety of functions. Two functions, at least during this century, have dominated. It has served business by identifying, sorting, and developing talent and by inculcating work values, and schooling has been the protector of the American dream. Schools have been the means for some young people to get ahead and for justifying the lack of success of others. In hard economic times, with high unemployment and an uncertain future, the importance of these functions increases as options for getting ahead and making a place in the world collapse, especially for the least favored in our society.

During such times, competition increases. Young people compete with one another not only for grades, but for future opportunities, and much hinges on how well they do in school. Very slight differences in performance may open or close doors to opportunity, of which there are far too few to go around. In college, perhaps the worst, or best, example is what happens in the competition to be admitted into medical school, where there are very few slots and many able students seeking to fill them. When the stakes are high, and young people are beginning to learn very early how high the stakes are, few if any risks will be taken. There is simply no room for failure. Rewards come to those able and willing to conform to the good student ideal. Those who are not, get what they deserve. Anxious parents know this well and press the ideal on their children and on teachers too. They know that in the race to get ahead, those who cannot conform fall by the wayside. Only the strong (and perhaps the uninteresting) survive.

The need to educate vast numbers of students efficiently, to socialize them, and to sort them fairly into what was viewed as their appropriate social positions — girls to be mothers and secretaries; boys to be laborers, businessmen, mechanics and public figures — encouraged adoption of a factory view of education when the public school system was created.[8] Initially, the notion was that everyone would go through the same school experience and talent would rise to its own level. Ideally, all youngsters would become used to working within a large and complex institution and develop the social skills and work habits essential to success within such organizations. These skills and habits were understood as serving both the needs of the individual student and the national interest. Standardization, as a means for achieving both efficiency and fairness, was understood as a necessity. Gradually, the institution and the roles it prescribed solidified into what we know today as school, where teaching and learning play second fiddle to administrative convenience and where orderliness is cherished above all else.

The way schools are built, the resources disseminated, the day organized, the students allocated to classrooms, and the rewards bestowed, shape teacher and student behavior. Both are domesticated. Young people come to be "viewed", in John Goodlad's terms, "only as students, valued primarily for their academic aptitude and industry rather than as individual persons."[9] They learn how to deal with "crowds, praise and power" and develop a remarkable tolerance for "delay, denial, interruption, and social distraction" that spills out, even for the best of students, into other aspects of life, particularly the political and economic.[10] Passivity is rewarded, conformity honored. Through their school experience, young people are well prepared to become organization men and women, but certainly *not* well prepared for the kind of bold and intelligent risk taking, or even thoughtful cooperation, that is essential to a vital society. Moreover, talent withers under a system that encourages students and teachers to come to accept life spent "in a state of spectatorship."[11]

In an important small book, *The Paideia Proposal*, by Mortimer Adler, the case is made that in order for young people to be educated they need school experiences of different kinds.[12] Adler asserts, quite rightly, that they need to be coached in the development of skills in mathematics, reading, writing as well as in athletics. The selection of the term "coaching" was felicitous. One learns to play basketball well through not only playing basketball, but also through having one's performance carefully critiqued by someone who understands the nuances of the game much better than we do. A master should teach us. We need to think of developing intellectual skills in the same way.

The development of skills in writing, understood essentially as the process of thinking, requires coaching. Students have the right to receive careful, thoughtful, and critical feedback on their work. To do this, teachers must have time to provide such feedback, which clearly requires smaller class sizes than are now common. In addition, teachers, themselves, must be able writers; they must have developed an ear for language and a knowledge of its uses. Furthermore, teachers must know how to give assignments and criticism in ways that stimulate students to write, rather than crush the desire out of them, as is so often the case when writing is product oriented — a single paper representing the sum of required written work for a term.

Lecturing in order to develop skills, other than notetaking and listening, makes absolutely no sense at all. It is, however, a reasonably effective way, when done well, to convey to students large amounts of information that would not be easily accessible in other ways. This is the second area of educational experience Adler thinks students require. Again, I quite agree. Unfortunately, as we have seen, teacher talk almost completely dominates the experience of students in school and helps instill in them a variety of less than desirable traits. Teachers should not stop lecturing, but a better understanding of the strengths and weaknesses of this approach to instruction needs to be developed so that lecturing will no longer be expected to carry educational burdens it cannot possibly bear. There is an implicit message given to parents, teachers, and students in how our schools are organized: the message is that teaching is synonymous with lecturing; good teachers are good lecturers. The reduction of teaching to lecturing represents a destructive conceptual confusion that leads to many sorts of mischief.

Finally, Adler argues that all students should have the opportunity to engage in Socratic dialogue on issues of enduring human concern and to draw upon a variety of carefully selected texts. Once again, the challenge is to rethink the kinds of experiences we offer the young under the heading of education and to reconsider the organizational structure we have created to provide these experiences. The structure has succeeded in making it nearly impossible for teachers to provide some of the kinds of experiences they know are most educative. Obviously, though Socratic dialogue can take place in classes containing twenty-five or thirty-five students, its effectiveness is severely constrained. Ten to fifteen students is a much more reasonable number. Also, Socratic dialogue cannot take place around programmed readers that make a virtue out of limited vocabularies.

Indirectly, Adler is telling us that we get precisely the kinds of students we should expect, in view of the types of experiences we offer them in school. Given the high priority placed on lecturing it is hardly surprising that our "better" students would be those who learn how to listen most effectively and to regurgitate what they are told are the facts. Given the high priority placed on getting ahead, it should not surprise anyone that our better students learn quickly how to manipulate the system to their ends. And, given our belief that proof of success is getting a high-status, well-paying job, it should not surprise us that nonvocational arguments for learning fall on deaf ears.

Although school critics have paid comparatively little attention to the quality of life teachers have in school, it is also apparent that, for the most part, we get precisely the kinds of teachers we deserve — ones who can survive within a confining and intellectually uninteresting environment dominated by routine and consumed with problems of managing students. Fortunately, we also have a goodly number of very fine teachers who are able to find and exploit a sufficient number of cracks within the walls of the institution that they are able to take a few risks in the name of education. But it is unreasonable to place our hopes for better education on the backs of these persons who are able to carry out their good works in part because they withdraw behind the security of a closed and windowless classroom door. They are isolated, and, as a result, comparatively powerless. Their actions do, however, remind us that alive in the minds of many teachers are exciting visions of educational possibility that await fruition, and this is cause for hope.

When planning opportunities for students to engage in Socratic dialogue we must learn to accept, even honor, false starts and errors honestly made. If we cannot do this, then the potential virtue of this approach to education will be lost in the celebration of right answers, produced without attention to any other validity claims than those of established authority. Dialogue must not be reduced to monologue. Similarly, when we consider how to coach young people in the development of skills of various kinds, whether they be intellectual or athletic, it is the process of skill development, more than the product, that ought to be of primary concern, at least initially. The diagnosis of error and the providing of useful feedback and suggestions, not necessarily prescriptions, for improvement is essential. Young people must have an abundance of opportunities to practice their skills, to study exemplars so that they can develop and internalize models worthy of emulation by which they may eventually judge the quality of their own work, and to talk about their work in the light of the progress they are making with others similarly engaged. They must be enabled to see that with practice, they can and do get better.

In coaching and in Socratic dialogue, young people should come face to face with their limitations and be pressed to go beyond them. In order for this to happen, our schools must become much more secure places than they are currently — secure, not so much in the sense of being free from the fear of physical attack, but free from the fear that to make a mistake is somehow to be flawed. As has been noted, this is hardly the case currently. For good students a mistake is a failure. At every turn they seek to discover precisely what the teacher wants so they can deliver it. While good students find and plod along the established pathways to assured success through remarkable conformity, bad students give up for reasons that seldom have anything to do with lack of innate ability.

Adler's emphasis is on students gaining needed background information, skills, and the ability to reflect. He ignores one other essential aspect of education: the opportunity to act within and upon the public world, the opportunity to function as a citizen.[13] There are two reasons for providing young people with such opportunities: to help them understand the public world, and to develop the skills, attitudes, and values essential for enriching it. Understanding requires that young people be given opportunities to actively engage the public world, to study, and to shape it. One of the major failings of the public school is that it has been essentially disconnected from the public world, which, when it is studied at all, is viewed at a distance. Rather than participate in political campaigns, for example, students read about them. Rather than study the impact of social class differences within their communities, they interpret income distribution graphs in textbooks.

Of the attitudes needed to enrich the public world, commitment, social sensitivity, compassion, and empathy stand out. These are qualities that are crushed by the quest for attaining a competitive edge. Nevertheless, they are qualities that ought to pervade all that is done in the school, from building administration to curriculum decision making. In addition, specific activities designed to foster their development within young people should be provided. I noted that McKenzie and a few of the other scholarship applicants listed on their vitas involvement in service activities. Whether they engaged in such activities in order to increase the likelihood of obtaining scholarships or because they genuinely were concerned about other people, I cannot say for certain. I believe, however, their concern was genuine, which sets these few young people apart from the rather bleak views presented in *Higher Education and the American Resurgence*. Whatever the case, these young people listed on their vitas (or mentioned) that they were engaged in good works of various kinds — helping the elderly in rest homes, for example. Not all, to be sure, had experiences of this kind, but quite a few did. Moreover, in aspiring to be teachers they knew they could not expect to do very well financially; their hope was to make a difference in the lives of others.

Unfortunately, my suspicion is that in good measure these values developed in spite of, not because of, these students' experience of schooling. They likely are products of deeply engrained religious or cultural values that emphasize the importance of nurturing and service. Emphatically, the schools ought to encourage these values.

Building into the school experience opportunities for service of various kinds is essential if we are to help form young people who are not only effective problem solvers and literate risk takers but who are also decent and compassionate citizens.[14] Opportunities of this kind need not be confined to working in rest homes, although that kind of contribution is surely valuable. The key element is that young people must have the opportunity to come to see themselves as connected to a larger human world that is characterized by immense suffering, and remarkable triumphs. In this world, within and without the family, they have parts to play, and how well or how poorly they play them makes a difference. Opportunities must be provided for all young people to become deeply involved in the lives of others; they must come to recognize that we are all interconnected and interdependent.

My own public school teaching experience in an interdisciplinary program designed for "bad" students provides an example. Perhaps the most successful learning activity I ever planned was one that involved a few ninth through twelth graders, who were having a difficult time in school, in teaching reading at a nearby elementary school to first and second graders who themselves were having a difficult time. My students saw they could make a difference, and it felt good to them. Once allowed to get outside of narrow self-interest, they began to see themselves as capable and responsible members of the human community.

What are schools about? Schools are about producing good students. But it is time that we begin thinking very carefully about the qualities we allow our good students to develop, just as we ought to continue to be concerned about the qualities of bad students. Young people require a different set of educational experiences than we currently provide for them. This is not to say that many good things do not happen in schools, for they certainly do. Some young people do learn how to take risks, some learn how to think very well, some become increasingly compassionate, and some become politically involved. Such students are, however, exceptions. When these exceptional young people come along, as they occasionally do, and survive initial screenings for scholarships, we ought to take great care in how we handle them, for they deserve to be cherished and encouraged.

But, cherishing a few nonconformist oddballs is not enough. Universities and colleges ought to begin rethinking their standards for admission and for scholarships so that the exception can become the rule. If we want young people to be risk takers, if we want them to be politically engaged, if we want them to be compassionate and caring, then we ought to be rewarding these qualities in addition to those we associate with academic performance. There is much more to being a good student than the ability to obtain good grades and high test scores.

3

Sorting and Labeling

I N Frank Baum's book, *The Wizard of Oz*, a rather remarkable thing happens to Dorothy Gale.[1] From the movie we remember the general outline of the story: Dorothy, the young, wide-eyed innocent from Kansas, has the amazing experience of being caught in a tornado that drops her and Auntie Em's house on top of the Wicked Witch of the East somewhere over the rainbow in the fairy land of Oz. Because of her deed, Dorothy is taken by the local inhabitants, strange, small people, called Munchkins, to be a powerful sorceress. Dorothy does not think of herself in any way other than that of being a lost little girl far away from the security of home. While still recovering from her abrupt landing, Dorothy meets and is kissed by Glinda, a genuine sorceress of great power. We return to the book for the rest of the story.

Glinda's kiss has an importance unknown to Dorothy; it marks her as being under Glinda's protection. The Wicked Witch of the West does not know Dorothy is protected when she calls upon the flying Monkey King and commands him and his army to destroy Dorothy and her companions: Nick Chopper (the Tin Woodman), the Scarecrow, and the Cowardly Lion. The Scarecrow's stuffings are spread about and he ends up hanging in a tree. Nick is thrown down a chasm and badly mangled. The Cowardly Lion is caged. But, when the monkeys swoop down to lift Dorothy to a certain death, they see the mark. They cannot do their mistress' bidding, and instead return to the cas-

tle with Dorothy. The Witch also recognizes the mark but realizes that Dorothy is unaware of it. She terrorizes the child in the
vain hope that she will be able to obtain the magical silver shoes
(not ruby slippers) that her sister had been wearing when the sky
fell upon her. The child believes the Witch can hurt her, even
though the Witch knows full well she cannot. It is a cruel bluff.
We all know how the story ends but the reason it ends happily is
not primarily a matter of Dorothy's skill with a pail of water.
Rather, it is because of the kiss and its meaning to those who
recognized its mark. Because of the mark Dorothy's life was
changed dramatically.

Students have marks of various kinds. Some labels are
more or less of their making, and they wear them proudly
whether spiked orange-and-black hair, or designer jeans. There
are "punkers," "cowboys," "jocks," and all sorts of other student clusterings. But, other labels are more like Dorothy's; the
bearer is not even aware of them. Some students are labeled
"gifted," others "emotionally disturbed." Still others are labeled
"unmotivated," or are "overachievers." The list of such labels is
endless, each one purportedly reflecting accurately a small slice
of the diversity that is humanity. What they have in common is
that each reflects a set of institutional priorities, and brings with
it a set of assumptions about the nature of those so labeled, an
established mode of treatment, and a set valuation.

Teachers and administrators must deal with large numbers
of students; in thinking about them, in planning their programs,
and in counseling them, categories must be used; it is unavoidable. However, what categories are used, and how they are used
and understood, may vary dramatically depending on institutional aims, cultural values, and personal bias.

The categories of schooling primarily reflect the aim of
sorting young people and, simultaneously, the importance of
meeting individual needs and serving individual interests. There
is a fundamental tension here that is resolved by how the word
"needs" is defined institutionally. Needs are almost always understood as lacks—the task is to find out what a young person
cannot do, when he or she is supposed to be able to do it, as
determined by a statistical norm, like grade level.[2] In the name
of meeting student needs, young people are categorized and

placed in programs that offer widely differing opportunities to become educated; it is all done for the love of children and in the knowledge of what is best for them.

Educators are helped in their task of sorting and labeling by educational researchers who have devoted themselves to producing ever finer categories by which to distinguish among young people, and ever better means for overcoming deficits. They have done this because of a commitment to the analysis and categorization of differences—the spirit of nineteenth-century biological science still lives. The researcher's professional status is closely tied to how effective they are in convincing educators of the reality of their categories and the worth of their treatments. Once created, an army of researchers and graduate students quickly begins discovering ever better ways of pigeonholing young people to make certain that the right students are put in the right places; psychological testing instruments of various kinds, combined with clinical interviews, are frequently used to determine where a student belongs. At the extreme, test results alone determine placement; educational judgements are not even necessary, tests decide it all.

Once a category becomes part of the language and culture of educators, once it is institutionalized, it takes on a life of its own. It is as though the label used is actually the person to whom it has been assigned. Knowingly or not, once marked, teachers may interact with what they know about the category into which a child is placed, rather than the child with whom they are working. The category mediates interaction, and the child is neatly stereotyped.

A child is greeted by schooling categories upon first registering for kindergarten. The afternoon kindergarten in many locations is for children who do not know their colors, are not reading ready, and do not know their numbers. These children are in need of remediation. The morning kindergarten is for children who have these skills and understanding. So, even before school begins, we have the makings of "slow" and "fast" learner categories.

Initially, the categories that confront young people are gross ones, but they become finer and more powerful very early. By the conclusion of first grade, relatively permanent reading groups are formed, sometimes with euphemistic names; children are Eagles, Bluebirds, and Robins — above, at, or below grade level.

When the numbers of students having similar needs and, sometimes, interests is very large, tracks are created for them so that they may be handled in similar ways. That is, it is accurate to say that children are fitted to the tracks available to them. This is done under the assumption that this is the most cost effective, efficient, way of educating young people. It is also considered the natural and proper means of serving individual differences. When only a few students fit a category, and they are highly visible, or their parents highly vocal (a category on the rise is Learning Disabled Gifted!), small programs are organized, but most often, differences are handled informally, usually within individual classrooms. Being placed in a track is part of the educational experience of virtually all American public school students; all of us who have graduated from public schools have been tracked because all schools track in English, math, and science.[3]

There are two general types of tracking. The first is whole school tracking, in which the school program is divided into various pathways toward graduation: college, general, and vocational preparation. The second type of tracking is composed of divisions that are made within programs — everyone takes history, for example, but some courses are identified as honors, or basic. Both types are based upon the same set of educational assumptions. The first assumption is that "students learn better when they are grouped with other students who are considered to be like them academically — with those who know about the same things, who learn at the same rate, or who are expected to have similar futures." The second is that "students, especially the slower ones, feel more positively about themselves and school when they are in homogeneous groups." The third is that "student track placements are appropriate, accurate, and fair." Finally, the fourth is that "teaching is easier (with respect to both meeting individual needs and managing classroom instruction in general) when students are in homogeneous groups."[4] None of these assumptions hold up well under scrutiny, with the possible exception of the fourth in which the word,"easier," gives rise to some difficulty.

Let us consider each in turn. Do students learn better when homogeneously grouped? There is a powerful common sense to ability grouping. It makes such good sense to put young people who are alike together. But common sense often leads us astray. For the most part, it appears that students who are identified as most able do no better, or just slightly better, when isolated from their less able peers, but those at the bottom do decidedly worse in achievement.

There are good reasons for this result. In class, people of lower socio-economic status tend to be given fewer opportunities to engage in high-quality content than their better off peers. They also do less homework. It should not, therefore, surprise us that these young people, and minorities, are disproportionately represented in lower tracks. Fewer opportunities to learn, spread out over an extended period of time, result in lower levels of achievement; conversely, more and better quality opportunities to learn, given over an extended period of time, result in higher levels of achievement. Good teaching is also usually more evident in higher tracks than in lower. Those behaviors that researchers have shown to correlate with improved student learning — teacher enthusiasm, clarity and variability, and high-task orientation — are more likely to show up in the classes taken by high-track students.

Teacher expectations also differ: teachers expect more and higher quality work from higher track students than they do from lower track students. An example comes to mind. Recently I worked with a student teacher placed in a working-class school. One afternoon she gave an assignment to her world history class that required that they do some independent library research. They were used to sitting and taking notes in anticipation of an examination on the facts; this was something new and unexpected. Just as she completed giving the assignment to the class her cooperating teacher, a well-intentioned and very popular fellow, piped up saying, "You can't expect these kids to do that; they can't do it." She was dumbfounded, she did not know that, nor believe it, but he turned out to be right. He was correct in that they most certainly would not do it, which he took to mean they could not. "Would not" or "could not," it was all the same to him. My student found a small measure of hope in those few pupils who attempted the assignment, despite the warning that frustration was certain to follow, because they were able to complete it successfully. The rest believed their teacher—why should they try to do something they had been told was impossible? There is some truth to the statement that if a person keeps being told he or she is stupid, stupidity follows.

But what about gifted students, is it not true that they do much better when separated from their slower peers? Not so, but there is another issue here: do they need a different kind of education that requires that they be separated from their less able peers?

To date, the most important study of programs for the gifted is *Educating Able Learners: Programs and Promising Practices.*[5] The study takes for granted that good education is dependent upon homogeneous grouping, that different kinds of young people require fundamentally different kinds of education.[6] The body of the report, however, albeit indirectly and unintentionally, casts doubt upon this assumption. After reading the report the only reasonable conclusion that can be drawn is that there are few significant differences between the educational needs (there is that word again) of the child labeled gifted and the less able child.

A few quotes will illustrate the point. The formula for success of a program designed primarily for "potentially gifted children" from low-income families, ages two to eight, is to "catch them young, work with their parents, and provide a rich educational program in a creative environment. Then watch the children blossom into independent, productive young people."[7] Of course, but all children deserve such an opportunity. In reference to AP (Advanced Placement) courses the report states that students think "more rigorous courses don't necessarily require more time" than less rigorous classes. Why? Because "they find the AP teachers more skilled in giving thoughtful assignments and less inclined to mete out busywork."[8] Again, all children deserve competent teachers, ones able to give thought-provoking assignments. The report stresses the value of being placed in courses with motivated students. As one McArthur Fellow put it, "With the terrible teachers . . . the support of other students helped. In high school I think it helped to be surrounded by other academically interested students."[9] If this is good for able learners, is it not of even greater importance for the less able? Is there no possibility for so-called slow students to be academically interested students? Clearly, the presence of academically interested students is desirable in all classrooms. Perhaps there are not enough academically interested students to go around, which may be one unpleasant outcome of tracking, because low-track programs cultivate disengagement from learning.

Educators should "offer program options that reach through and beyond the normal institutional boundaries: across disciplines, across grade levels, and across levels of intelligence." They should also "encourage independence through projects that culminate in real products and employ the methods of inquiry used by real scholars."[10] There is no reason why these recommendations, and virtually all others presented, ought not to be part of every child's school program. If the educational requirements for all students are roughly the same, as I believe them to be, then perhaps we should wonder about the wisdom of continuing the practice of grouping young people homogeneously.

At present it appears as though giftedness more than anything else has become an avenue for aggressive parent groups, and special interest groups within the educational establishment (experts whose status depends on getting Americans to buy into their categories), for obtaining additional resources, resources that must come from somewhere, or more accurately, from someone.[11] Part of the reason the case is now being heard is that it plays on fears that America is becoming a second-rate power because the talents of a very few able learners are presumably being squandered.

One point made in the study that needs stressing is that no one quite knows what it means to be gifted, or talented. In practice, a high test score, teacher recommendations based upon student motivation to achieve, and strong parental support are what usually qualifies a student for special programs. Because of this situation, the authors argue that a much wider net needs to be thrown when attempting to identify promising young people: "We must recognize that not only are there many kinds of abilities but that each spans a continuum. No natural break in the continuum separates gifted students from others in any one ability or in collective abilities."[12] And, they oppose rigid definitions of giftedness. "So long as a rigid screening is used to exclude students, some will be denied access to educational experiences because they just miss the cutoff. But if, as we suggest, the criteria for inclusion are made flexible, then no one should be denied access to programs that will serve their needs."[13] Under the right conditions, with sufficient resources and a national commitment to developing talent in its many forms, the net would draw in nearly all young people and there would be almost no reason whatsoever to have separate programs.

The second assumption is that students feel better about themselves and school when homogeneously grouped. Particularly for the lower track students, this assumption is not only false, it is pernicious. The belief is that less able young people should be protected from failure and from embarrassing themselves by doing stupid things in front of their more able peers; the reality is that they will be helped to accept mediocre performance even when they may be capable of performing much better. In fact, students in the lower tracks develop consistently poorer attitudes toward themselves and schooling. They feel that their classmates are unfriendly.[14] There is more yelling, fighting, hostility, and arguing in their classes. They feel disconnected and apathetic toward school, and they have fewer caring relationships with teachers. In short, school is not a pleasant place for low-track students and they leave in large numbers as a result — why should they stay when they are not welcome?

Labels and tracking go together. Presumably labels are merely descriptive of genuine student differences. In actuality, however, they reflect institutional evaluations of student worth. But, like Dorothy, it is not necessary for a student or teacher to recognize a label to possess it and enjoy or suffer its consequences. The power of tracking is that students know that others like them, their friends, are in the same boat, so how they are treated is likely to be perceived by them as how they should be treated. The student's perception, then, is that they deserve what they get; the institution only responds to their nature. This is important because it suggests that schools likely confirm the self-perceptions of lower-class students as somehow inferior to others, or those of gifted students that they are superior.

The third assumption is that student track placements are appropriate, accurate, and fair. This assumption is fraught with difficulty. As noted, homogeneous ability grouping frequently begins in kindergarten. If we were to make comparisons of the children enrolled in morning kindergartens (where such placements reflect tracking decisions) with children placed in afternoon kindergartens, we would find that a large number of the afternoon kids would be younger than the morning youngsters. Differences in maturity, not in ability, frequently result in initial placement differences. A child born in November or December, just after the cutoff date for admission into school, may actually be nearly a year older than a child born just prior to the final cutoff date; a year in the life of an adult may not be very significant developmentally, but for a child beginning school it may represent a very significant advantage, or disadvantage. These differences become very serious indeed when it is realized that the odds are overwhelming that a child placed in the bottom reading group in first grade will never be able to crack the top group even given twelve years of schooling to try. Initial placements tend to become permanent; movement between tracks is unlikely and becomes progressively more difficult as a student continues in school.

Students are misplaced for other reasons as well. Even using the best instruments available, estimates are that at least 10 percent of all young people are placed incorrectly. [15] For young people fortunate enough to be misplaced upwardly, the result is often a happy one: the children experience higher achievement than otherwise would have resulted. Why? Because they are exposed to teachers who expect more, are given the opportunity to mix with brighter, more stimulating peers, and because their self-perception and motivation to learn are greater.

When considering whether or not a placement is appropriate, the discussion usually centers on the probability that the student's needs are likely to be met. Recall, needs are deficiencies that someone, or something (a test), has noted. Assigning a need, therefore, is not a neutral act; to the contrary, it is political gesture that carries with it an implicit definition of what human beings ought to be like. Determining the appropriateness of a placement depends on the social purposes of education. When our aims are to enhance the public world and to expand the opportunities for individuals to participate within it, appropriateness requires that students be given opportunities to interact in significant ways with others representing diverse backgrounds and abilities. Given these aims, homogeneous grouping is not appropriate except in very extreme problem cases, and perhaps in the eleventh and twelfth grades in a few select subject areas — mathematics, foreign language (as currently taught) and the sciences — and to a limited degree within heterogeneously grouped classrooms.

Placements have a tendency to become more accurate and appropriate the longer an individual is in them. So, even if a child is misplaced initially, the odds are that, as teachers and others interact with him or her through the label, the child will come to fit the pigeonhole into which they have been placed, justifying not only the placement, but also the reality of the label itself. One result is that by the time a young person enters the secondary school, patterns of behavior and expectation are well estabished and very resistant to change. These patterns are so resilient that they acquire the appearance of being natural, real. When this happens it is no longer necessary for teachers to attend to the child as a source of data; the category that includes expectations for student behavior and prescriptions for remediation is all that is important to the educational institution — the label is the child.

The fourth assumption is that teaching is easier when students are in homogeneous groups. As noted, the word "easier" is the key to this assumption. Teachers would immediately agree that it does make a difference to have classes composed of young people of similar understanding and ability. But, they hold to this view because they take for granted current institutional arrangements, definitions of teaching (teaching as telling), of learning (learning as vessel filling), and the aims of schooling. When pressed they quickly admit, however, that even in the most carefully grouped classes they teach there still exists a remarkable range of ability, most of which is ignored. Indeed, the highest tracks are the most diverse.[16] The issue then is how wide a range of differences teachers will be required to address, and how they will address it.

To limit homogeneous grouping requires reconceptualizing teaching, learning, and education. Education must be viewed as a community responsibility in which students, teachers, and parents all have parts to play. Rather than emphasize competition among individuals, or individualization of the type in which students work alone on teacher assigned tasks, classes should be viewed as groups of persons responsible for one another's learning. Reflecting actual life relationships, students should become teachers; teachers should become students; parents and grandparents should becomes students and teachers.

In this regard, a cooperative, team, approach to learning has some real promise, as demonstrated by researchers at the University of Minnesota and Johns Hopkins University. The assumption is that students will learn best when they are working with one another in small, carefully selected, heterogeneous groups that exploit the potential of student-to-student interaction for learning—which is, for the most part, currently ignored, even avoided. Small groups work on a task, a project, product, or outcome, such as gaining a high group achievement average on a particular learning assignment. The group is rewarded for the quality, sometimes quantity, of its work based upon a preestablished standard.

The "essential elements of a cooperative learning structure" are, therefore,"a group goal and criterion-referenced evaluation system, and a system of rewarding group members on the basis of group performance."[17] Although this approach cannot bear the entire burden of instruction, evidence supporting its effectiveness is very encouraging: academic achievement is increased, students feel better about themselves and school, and have better interpersonal and intergroup relationships.

Far too little attention is given to the labels used in schooling, and to the costs of continuing our practice of sorting young people. Because educators and parents take sorting and labeling for granted, we rarely ask questions about them. We never ask, for example, to what educational labels actually refer. Is there really any such thing as an unmotivated young person? Or, is it only that we have a group of students who refuse to do what teachers want them to do, while they are at the same time working their tails off toward accomplishing some other set of purposes? What, pray tell, is an underachiever or an overachiever? How do we know that one child is not achieving his or her potential or, oddly enough, why should we be concerned if a child has exceeded his or her potential (as if that is possible)? Similar questions can be asked of all of the commonly used labels: emotionally disturbed, learning disabled, lazy, disaffected, hostile, passive, gifted, average (on grade level), potential dropout, honors student, *ad infinitum*.

Moreover, we ought to ask what it is these labels do for us educationally? What do they tell us about young people that is of any educational importance whatsoever? The one use that is apparent is distasteful: labels help justify, without explaining, school failure. They are a means of shifting the burden of failure onto students, while discouraging adult consideration of the origin of the problems. They help protect the institution from attack: students who have difficulty in school are declared aberrant, which means the challenge they may present to the institution is not legitimate, just as the testimony of a "crazy" person is suspect in court. Not all is hopeless, however. There are occasional exceptions to this generalization when educators pay careful attention to the student beneath the label in the attempt to diagnose particular learning problems. In such cases the aim is not to pigeonhole a student, but to understand and pinpoint the source of difficulty.

The labels of schooling make reform difficult. In part this is because labels make it unnecessary to think about education. They make it unlikely that counselors, teachers, administrators, and even parents (who especially love labels like "gifted"), will carefully attend to the student experience of schooling, or the teacher experience, for that matter. Labels are also applied to teachers, and they frequently obscure problems and issues. "Burnout" is a good example. Rather than call attention to difficult and demoralizing work conditions, use of the "burnout" label focuses attention on the individual teacher's inability to hold up under extraordinary pressure. Labels allow us to avoid problems, to define them without actually dealing with them.

To change schooling means changing the categories we use to think about and discuss young people. As long as we accept efficiency and sorting as primary educational aims, there is little reason to question the labels we use; they are effective means for these purposes. But I do not believe most educators hold these values as primary. They are accepted unreflectively, habitually. First and foremost, educators care about young people, and if they reflected on the quality of the educational experience students receive and are committed to improving it, then the evil of our labels and the system of tracking that produces them will come into stark contrast. Rather than seek to maintain labels that separate individuals, we must seek a language that expresses a high value for cooperation and involvement within and commitment to improving our public world. Currently we have no such language. As we become sensitive to the politics of language in the same sense that feminists have sensitized Americans to the prejudice in our use of pronouns, for example, our thinking can and will change, which is essential to fundamental school reform.

4

Excellence and Testing

EDUCATORS in each of the fifty states are busy responding to the challenge of making the schools excellent. Credits required for graduation in "solid" subjects are up, and less time is being spent on so-called frills. Definitions of these solid courses, say, English, are being shored up; too many silly classes have been masquerading as substantive. As a result, students who have any inkling of attending college are finding that they had better shape up and begin planning their programs early and well.

On the face of it, these are good changes; students should be taking more math, science, and English. But there is something more than a little disquieting about our response to the current crisis in public education. There has been surprisingly little discussion of what American schools are for or of what is meant by excellence; these are taken for granted. In the haste to reform, I fear we have bought into solutions without adequately attending to the problem that exists. Excellence in pursuit of an unworthy aim is certain to worsen our situation. Yet, excellence is the banner around which reformers of all shades have gathered. Excellence for what?

One way of understanding how excellence is being perceived, educationally, is to consider how the school problem has been defined. For the moment, but only for the moment, I will accept the view that American public education is terrible and that this is the root problem. The evidence usually presented of educational failure boils down to two basic assertions: too many Americans are functionally illiterate and, when compared to the students of other nations, our students score frightfully low on standardized achievement tests. *A Nation At Risk* made good use of this data, as have many of the two hundred plus reports on American education that have followed since its publication. Because of our method of gathering data, the first assertion can be easily collapsed into the second: the problem with American education is that our test scores are not high enough. From this conclusion, a jump is made: if test scores do not improve, America will quickly become a second-class power. At the risk of over-simplification, the assumption seems to be that there is a direct correspondence between test scores and economic and political power. High scores lead to greater power; low scores to less power.

It is not surprising that in America test scores should have received so much attention. We have had a long fascination with testing, and social scientists have long relished calling test scores to our attention when it has suited their political purposes, as for example, when seeking data to justify immigration quotas in the early 1920s.[1] We are mystified by the process of test construction and stand in awe of the experts who produce and interpret them. For the most part, we accept these experts' claims of the objectivity of testing.

Only in the last twenty or so years has anything approaching a critical public discourse about testing and the use of test data existed. But, even now many of us stubbornly hold to the value of testing, especially when it confirms that our children are brighter than other people's children and therefore deserving of special treatment. Given this fascination, falling test scores indicate that something is wrong at the very center of our being, and alarm follows.

There are other reasons why we take test scores as the primary means for determining student and school performance that deserve mention. In a competitive political and economic world, a world of scarcity, test scores offer a convenient, wonderfully and frightfully simple, way of making comparisons between groups. One need not understand the subtleties of testing to feel secure in asserting that high is good and low is bad. All that is necessary, for instance, to set policymakers on edge are two figures, one representing the math scores of ten-year-olds in the Soviet Union, and the other the scores of American fourth graders. The higher Soviet composite score becomes the standard of excellence. Similarly, test scores offer a convenient and, we assume, fair and objective means for making comparisons between and among individuals. We believe they establish merit, and we are very interested in rewarding merit. Once again, high is good, and low is bad, and young people are sorted within our schools accordingly. Based upon test scores, the more meritorious receive a very different kind of education from that offered to their less test worthy peers.

From a factory or marketplace view of schooling, test scores offer a simple and supposedly accurate measure of educational efficiency. The assumption is that they are a good way of determining whether or not we are obtaining the most for our educational dollar. We want a high quality product, produced as cheaply as possible; the test scores are taken as indicators of product quality and the worth of our investment. In some respects, standardized test scores function much like the Dow-Jones averages. We expect high returns and, if we do not get them, we consider shifting our resources, firing the board of directors, or forcing labor into making concessions.

Testing in America is very big business. To maintain itself as a growth industry, it is in the interest of testing corporations, like the giant Educational Testing Service with tax free revenues of 133 million dollars for fiscal 1983, to strengthen the view of Americans that standardized testing accurately and objectively determines student potential and is the best measure of student and school performance.[2] These corporations spend a tremendous amount of money to keep us from questioning the value of testing. They need not spend nearly that amount. Our faith in experts, our belief in the necessity of sorting young people, the simplicity of reporting, and our interest in making schools and teachers accountable in order to get the most out of the dollar, make many of us willing believers. There are, however, some serious dangers in being too willing believers. Let us take a closer look at testing, and at some of the assumptions commonly held about it.

Contrary to what most Americans believe, many, perhaps most, testing programs have little if anything to do with promoting student learning. Indications of this are readily available. For instance, test makers are consumed with the need to keep tests secure so that cheating will not take place — the tests ought to accurately indicate student performance. The claim is also made that test security helps keeps costs down by allowing use of items over extended periods of time. Forms A and B of the Stanford Achievement Test, for example, were copyrighted in 1972 and widely and profitably used until very recently. In fact, however, the events following passage of the New York state truth-in-testing bill, which requires that test questions and graded answer sheets be made available to students, suggests that increased costs have little if anything to do with test makers' passion for test security.[3] We have been duped. The more basic reason for the concern with security is not to minimize cheating, or to save money, rather it is to protect tests makers from having their products carefully scrutinized which inevitably leads to embarrassment.

Unfortunately, school districts and even state legislators have accepted, for the most part, that test security is essential to objectivity and to cost effectiveness. The South Carolina legislature, for example, actually considered passage of a "bill that would provide for fines of up to $1,000 or as much as 90 days in jail for teachers, principals or others convicted of permitting students access to test questions, releasing test booklets or answer keys, or otherwise breaching test security."[4] Aside from the unenforceability of such a law, one wonders, how serious test makers can be about promoting student learning when students in all but a few states are not even given knowledge of the items they missed?

Another indicator is how loosely tests are tied to the content taught. A large school district with which I am very familiar has invested tens of thousands of dollars in the use of the Stanford Achievement Test as the means of determining student competency. The test was administered for the first time three years ago and nearly 20 percent of the seniors failed one or more portions of the exam. The district administration was thrown into a tizzy. How could this be? To make matters worse, in one of the wealthiest high schools in the district, a school noted widely for its innovative programs and outstanding student achievement, the failure rate was over 25 percent. Quietly, behind the scenes, administrators began developing ways of lowering the failure rate, including offering special short-courses in test taking to students. What they realized was that the test did not accurately reflect the educational experience of those who had taken it: it lacked content validity, to use a testing phrase. By investing in the Stanford Achievement Test the district found itself in the unpleasant, but politically expedient, position of encouraging schools to alter the curriculum to better reflect the test. In short, they needed to make the test work, not for the purposes of facilitating student learning, but in order to establish the wisdom of the initial decision to invest in the testing program. In the meantime, however, students who do poorly on the examination are being told, in effect, that they are stupid.

The issue of the content validity of standardized tests has an additional aspect to it that ought to be of great importance to Americans. One wonders, given differences in political philosophy, if American and Soviet students ought to be scoring at the same levels as is widely assumed. Should not what goes on in American schools be in some ways very different from what goes on in Soviet schools? Put differently, is democratic education identical to education in a totalitarian state? I hope this is not so. If the school experience for American students ought to be different from the experience of any other group of students then, perhaps, we ought to expect our students to score differently on standardized tests.

This is a shocking idea, but worth considering. We know that there is a direct relationship between practice on test-related items and increase in test scores. Assuming that intelligence is spread equally throughout the world, the authors of *A Nation At Risk* are quite right; all that is necessary for American scores to compare favorably with those of Japan or the Soviet Union is to have our young people spend an amount of time equivalent to that spent by students in these countries practicing the operations upon which they will be tested. But this means that unless we are willing to extend the school day and year, which we apparently are not, then schooltime must be taken away from other activities that also may be of great worth to us as a nation. For instance, time spent in classrooms discussing what are commonly called "higher order questions"—questions that elicit from students opinions, judgements, and evaluations, rather than aim at obtaining right answers—actually is time wasted if the aim is to increase standardized test scores in which concentration on lower-order questions common to student drills has the greater payoff. But, the larger question is whether young people in a democracy should be spending so much time being drilled. Put differently, do the tests represent what we value most as a free people? If they do not, which I believe to be the case, then higher test scores may actually be indications of educational deterioration rather than improvement.

An additional word on content validity: teachers and administrators recognize that test scores reflect either positively or negatively on their performance. They also recognize that higher scores come from making certain that young people have the opportunity to practice the operations upon which they will be tested. Achieving high content validity may take many forms but, in practice, one approach dominates; that is, teachers teach to the test. The content validity is assured because the test becomes the curriculum.

To help teachers teach what is on the test, some testing agencies, while unwilling to distribute actual examinations, have written booklets of instructional objectives and sample questions. The instructional objectives tell the teachers what topics students will be tested on, and the sample questions let them know what the students will be doing to demonstrate their ability to meet the objectives. The Educational Testing Service, while falsely claiming that coaching will not appreciably affect student scores, sells booklets on how to take the Scholastic Aptitude Test and a paperback published by Scribner Book Company called *10 SATs,* which contains just what it says, ten tests.

Materials of this kind are put to good use. Two years ago I spent fall term observing a mathematics classroom in a junior high school. Two weeks before the students were scheduled to take a competency examination the department head passed out sample test questions to each of the teachers who then began drilling the students. For that two-week period the normal curriculum was put on hold. Because the students were used to testing and understood well the importance of doing their best, the change was taken in stride. Though the teachers were far from pleased at having their programs disrupted, they thought they had no other reasonable alternative. They knew that once the tests had been scored, the administration would let each of them know how well their students did in comparison with other classes and other schools. Although the principal made a point of telling the staff that he was not using the data to make judgements about teacher quality, they all believed that he did. Nothing he could have possibly said would have changed their minds. Moreover, the teachers also knew that the test data would be of virtually no use to them in either improving their instruction or in pinpointing student learning problems. The reason for the tests was to convince the public that their children were receiving a first rate education and the test scores proved it.

On first consideration, one might assume that sticking closely to a standardized text book would make certain that there is a good fit between the curriculum and test. This is hardly the case. A recent review of the relationship of the content of four widely used textbooks for fourth grade mathematics to that of four of the most commonly used standardized achievement tests including the Iowa Test of Basic Skills, the Stanford Achievement Test, the Metropolitan Achievement Tests, and The Comprehensive Tests of Basic Skills, showed a surprisingly poor match.[5]

In mathematics, one might assume that obtaining a close relationship would be relatively easy. But, it is not. The best fit was between the Metropolitan Achievement Tests and the Holt textbook in which the students had the opportunity of learning 50 percent of the topics upon which they would be tested. The worst fit was between the Houghton-Mifflin text and the Stanford Achievement Test in which the students only had the opportunity to study 21 percent of what would be tested. In short, even when using a text of recognized quality, students have virtually no assurance they are learning what counts. The odds are, in fact, that they know much more than the test shows, although they may also know a great deal less depending on how lucky they are in drawing questions.

Those who make judgements about student learning based upon test scores ought to be having second thoughts. A low test score may have virtually nothing to do with either poor instruction or lack of student motivation and interest, as is frequently assumed. Under such conditions, suspending use of a textbook in order to teach directly to a test makes good political sense. Whether or not it makes educational sense, and has anything to do with excellence, is another matter entirely.

Some tests, like the Scholastic Aptitude Test, which is used to make admissions decisions to college, actually make a virtue out of lack of content validity. Unlike achievement tests, which presumably sample what a student has learned by virtue of schooling, aptitude tests are supposed to get at something more general, inherent intellectual ability. To determine what this is (test makers are caught in a hopeless tautology: intelligence is knowing whatever tests test), test makers argue that examinations should be content free; they should not require specific content knowledge but rather, the demonstration of specific intellectual abilities. In fact, however, the difference between aptitude and achievement is virtually nonexistent; both sloppily measure opportunities to learn.

Obtaining a good fit between test content and the curriculum is compounded by the problem of cultural and social class bias, which further weakens test makers' claims to test objectivity. Students enter classrooms with widely different experiences. Those from better off families may have travelled widely, enjoyed a good library, and had parents who were able to read to them on a daily basis. The experience of poor children results in a very different set of background learning that affects school and standardized test performance. There is, for example, a direct positive relationship between parents' mean income and performance on the SAT (Scholastic Aptitude Test) test.[6] The more money a child's parents make, the greater the likelihood the child will do well on this test. Conversely, the poorer the family, the greater the likelihood the student will not do well. The quest to produce an examination that is insensitive to differences in social class and cultural background is hopeless. A high score says as much about the background of students and the fit of this background to tested items, as it does about the exellence of a school program.

A word should also be said about the nature of the content typically tested. I have before me a copy of the "Advanced Form E" of the Stanford Achievement Test copyrighted by Harcourt Brace Jovanovich in 1981. I also have the "Directions for Administering" the test battery forms E/F. This test represents the seventh revision: 1923, 1929, 1940, 1953, 1964, and 1973. If past trends continue, we can expect an eighth revision soon. The SAT is used primarily to test junior high age students, although it is also used by some districts in the high schools as a competency exam. Such exams are supposed to show what a student has learned while in school, and judgements are made based upon test results to determine if what has been learned is minimally satisfactory for the student to advance a grade or to graduate. Aggregate scores are used to make judgements about the quality of the schooling offered.

The test is composed of ten sections: Reading Comprehension, Vocabulary, Listening Comprehension, Spelling, Language, Concepts of Number, Mathematics Computation, Mathematics Applications, Science and Social Science. Given our current national interest in science, and my own interest in social science, I thought it would be interesting to analyze the kinds of intellectual operations required of students by these subtests. According to the "Directions for Administering," the science subtest is supposed to measure a student's understanding of the basic concepts of both the biological and physical sciences. In addition, students are supposed to demonstrate that they are able to use inquiry skills.

Can it be assumed that the test actually tests what the writers claim? A review of the sixty science items reveals that no fewer than fifty of them require only that the student know a simple fact, such as the definition of gene. Other items require that the student be able to read a graph or count. Where, one wonders, are the inquiry questions? A similar pattern is reflected in the social studies subtest in which the ability to recall facts accounts for forty-five of sixty items. The remaining fifteen items require that the student be able to read a map, apply definitions and make inferences from headlines. The domination of the tests by items requiring only factual knowledge and the requirement that each test be timed (thirty minutes are alotted to both the science and social science subtests) supports the conclusion of Kenichi Shibuya, a Japanese child psychologist, that the tests are good indicators of a "child's ability to memorize, to accumulate information and details" and little more.[7]

It is also worth noting that nine of the sixty items on the social studies subtest are clearly ambiguous, and a good case could be made that there is more than one correct answer. To obtain the right answer, it appears that students would necessarily need to share, with test makers, a set of basic assumptions about the political and economic world within which we live; obviously, not all students share this view. Question 26, for instance, asks the following: *Inventions that raise a society's level of technology also usually:*

    f. affect the society's religious beliefs
    g. decrease the society's educational level
    h. change the society's standard of living
    j. help to maintain the society's traditions

Having spent sufficient time to be able to think like test writers who are, for the most part, ordinary people, I am confident *h* is the correct answer. However, *f* is also certainly true. Unfortunately, we cannot have it both ways. At first glance, question 50 is a real puzzler: *Which group probably has the strongest traditions?:*

    f. A group of miners
    g. An established religious group
    h. Scientists working on a project
    j. A group of customers in a restaurant.

I suspect the correct answer is *g* because of use of the word "established." However, I know of a United Mine Worker's local that has deeply entrenched traditions, just as I am aware of how science becomes ritualized especially when tied to a long-term research project. And, with but a little stretch of my imagination, I recall my three years during high school working at the Red Carpet Restaurant where Greek traditions were everpresent. The importance of these items is that they are designed to discriminate between better and poorer students. Apparently, given the commitment to multiple choice testing and the difficulty of writing unambigious items that discriminate, ambiguity is inevitable. To sort students, test writers confuse and bewilder in the name of objectivity.

Content and content validity–related problems do not exhaust the difficulties encountered when using standardized test scores as the primary determiners of educational excellence. Two additional shortcomings deserve mention. The reporting of results in percentiles for comparative purposes washes out important differences within tested populations that may account for variations in test scores quite separate from whatever a school is doing. These differences may be products of culture or even physical or mental handicaps. Ignoring such differences, among other things, encourages teachers and administrators to alter programs when, in fact, a change may not be in order or a change of a different kind is required.

A recent example comes to mind. The parents of students in one Salt Lake City high school were up in arms when the district reported for the first time in fifteen years test score data for all four district high schools. A large, bold, headline followed release of the data: "Low scores dismay South High parents." The data suggested that the average ninth-grade student at South High School scored at the 39th percentile on the language portion of a standardized achievement exam, meaning that on average, South High School students were below average (50th percentile). Scores in the other content areas were, with the exception of mathematics, equally distressing. Parents were understandably very upset: "This was really a shock. I see this as evidence that South High School has got to get on the ball and come up with solutions."[8]

To make matters worse, students at the other high schools did very well scoring as high as the 85th percentile on the same language subtest. To calm parental concern, district and school-building administrators explained to school patrons that as a port-of-entry school South High School was unlike the other schools. Nearly a third of those who took the examinations were recent immigrants and had trouble with the English language. Unfortunately, when the scores were reported in aggregate form, and data was not available on how these students affected the overall standing of the school, parents were left with the certain feeling that the school was failing to educate their children. Subsequently, data were made available that showed that when the port-of-entry students' test scores were removed from the testing pool, South High School scores approximated the national average. The result was that rather than look upon the presence of a large number of foreign-born students as an educational blessing, it became, to the minds of many parents, a curse. In addition, a year later, aggregate test score data was used to help justify a decision to close South High (after the 1987–88 school year) rather than one of the other three high schools to effect sizeable financial savings through consolidation.

The goal of mitigating some of the differences between groups that lead to variations in test scores has lead a few educators, who take the value of testing for granted, to some remarkable conclusions. One researcher found, for example, after conducting a very interesting two-year observational study of the meaning of testing to Navajo elementary school-age children, that among the factors influencing test performance was that they did not understand testing in the same sense as did teachers, nor did they think testing very important. Rather, they understood "tests as game-like or non-serious events."[9] This view of testing likely affected how well the students did. The conclusion reached was that teachers should work harder to make certain that Navajo children learn the importance of testing — that is, teachers need to help Navajo children develop a healthy dose of test anxiety. But, one wonders, is it not more reasonable to raise questions about the desirability of testing in this situation and to begin exploring other ways of obtaining data useful for making instructional decisions, assuming, perhaps falsely, that the improvement of learning is the intention for testing. Extending this conclusion, are we interested in trying to follow the lead of the Japanese into *shiken jigoku* [examination hell]?

It certainly does have an effect on how seriously testing is taken and, most assuredly, on the scores achieved. But, is this educational excellence?

Finally, our commitment to mass and frequent testing has locked us into a testing format that itself is a source of many problems. In order to test literally millions of young people, it is necessary to produce examinations that are relatively inexpensive, and easily administered and scored. Moreover, the results must lend themselves to easy reporting and interpretation. The effect is that we are bound tightly to the use of multiple choice test items and computer scoring sheets. This form of testing lends itself best to testing factual knowledge, as we have seen from the analysis of the kinds of intellectual operations required of students by the Stanford Achievement Test, and not to higher order intellectual operations.

The techniques of test construction have improved little since their inception, and there is small reason to believe significant improvements will soon be forthcoming. We should be very cautious about what we expect from standardized testing and very reluctant to make conclusions about the quality of education offered to the young or on the quality of their learning, based primarily upon test data. Standardized tests are, in short, very poor measures of excellence of any kind except excellence in the ability to take tests which, in and of itself, is a skill of sorts.

The evidence that test taking is a skill, and that with practice scores can be increased, is overwhelming. David Owen describes the participation of students, who can afford the stiff fees, in courses specially designed to increase test scores. The Princeton Review course for the Scholastic Aptitude Test — the test most often referred to by those concerned with excellence because of the steady decline in scores from the mid–1960s until 1982 — costs five hundred dollars, but the results are impressive. Students taking the course average gains of about 185 points on the combined verbal and math scales (each scale goes from 200 to 800). With students who are very highly motivated the increase is closer to 250 points.[10] I wonder, in what sense are these young people any smarter? A change of this magnitude in a score has tremendous importance to students aside from the obvious benefit in self-esteem. If two students have the same high school grade point average, a difference of 200 points is about the difference between one student at the 33rd percentile and another at the 50th percentile of a college class.[11] Differences of this magnitude, and much smaller, may mean that a student either does or does not get into a preferred college where test scores are often taken very seriously. Similar courses exist to prepare students for the tests required for admission into professional schools.

Part of the success of courses on test taking comes from practicing items that are typically tested. For instance, students memorize the 150–word "Hit Parade" of words that most often show up on the verbal sections of tests. But a large portion comes from learning the tricks of test taking such as using the corner of the test booklet to measure angles in geometry drawings. More and more educators are coming to realize that testwiseness is an important skill to be taught. A 1979 survey of seven northeastern states, for example, found that a third of the high schools had special preparatory programs for the Scholastic Aptitude Test. Although these courses typically were electives, the credit received counted toward graduation.[12]

In the wake of our first national concern for educational excellence following the launching of Sputnik, John Gardner pressed the question in a small book: "Can we be Equal and Excellent Too?" He thought so. But, judging from the revision and publication in 1984 of a second edition of *Excellence*, we apparently did not learn our lesson the first time around. A central point of his argument is that as a people we must think of excellence in much broader terms than we usually do. There are, he says, many kinds of excellence even in the intellectual fields. "There is the kind of intellectual activity that leads to a new theory and the kind that leads to a new machine. There is the mind that finds its most effective expression in teaching and the mind that is most at home in research. There is the mind that works best in quantitative terms and the mind that luxuriates in poetic imagery."[13] Similarly, there are many kinds of excellence in the arts, in athletics, in crafts, in family life, and so on. Each arena of human endeavor has its own standards and excellence. The list is endless. Each historical period, he notes, rewards different types of excellence, and rewards differently. A person may be excellent in some area, but find that his or her particular excellence is not valued or is undervalued. If, as I fear, the excellence we reward is excellence in test taking, we are indeed in very serious trouble.

We are in trouble not only because the tests do not measure what they purport to measure, but because they emphasize, with the exception of numeracy and basic literacy, skills of little importance to building the public world, and because they are used to divide us in various ways and then to justify the divisions. A society, particularly a society that fancies itself democratic, must constantly press the question of whether or not excellence is valued and, if so, what kind of excellence. At present our vision is disturbingly constricted. We are choking ourselves in the celebration of excellence in test taking as though high test scores represent the essence of human achievement and the key to social progress.

We have been seduced; high test scores do not represent excellence in the broad sense. Rather, at best, high standardized test scores are indicators of excellence in an extraordinarily narrow slice of intellectual operations that certainly do not reflect the range of intellectual ability a society requires if it is to remain vital. Moreover, they are an incredibly flawed, even pernicious, means for determining the educational futures of our young people.

The authors of *A Nation At Risk* were quite right, excellence represents both a performance and an attitude. In order to judge the quality of a performance there must be publicly agreed upon standards. It is through encountering exemplars, in studying their lives and work, and then in striving to achieve a similar expression of human perfection that we internalize standards of excellence. This is so whether the endeavor is physics with Albert Einstein, poetry with Robert Burns, painting with my father, or teaching with my sister. By defining excellence narrowly, as a test score, we communicate a false message to the young that excellence represents a single performance, a state of being. This is not so. Burns's poems are not of equal merit; only occasionally did he attain the perfection we all recognize and celebrate.

The narrowness of this definition sends the message to

those who do not score well that they cannot achieve excellence. Excellence is a rarity because we encourage development of the attitude, even in the very young, that it is only within the reach of a gifted few who ought to occupy the highest occupational positions. This is nonsense except when excellence is narrowly and improperly construed. Gardner was correct, "The tone and fiber of our society depend upon a pervasive, almost universal striving for good performance. . . . We cannot have islands of excellence in a sea of slovenly indifference to standards."[14] Such an attitude can only develop when excellence is understood very broadly and honored accordingly. This is not possible if we are constantly on our knees before the testing idol.

To develop a broader view of excellence presents a difficult challenge to schools. As I have noted, there are great benefits to defining excellence narrowly, not the least among them being the ease of testing and the willingness of the public to take test scores as proof of school and student performance. In their more honest moments, teachers and school administrators know better. But they believe their hands are tied; at present, test scores form the language of educational discourse with the public.

As noted earlier, a critical discourse has been growing around standardized testing over the past twenty years. Although small, its existence is promising. Most attention has been given to IQ tests in part because of controversy surrounding the ridiculous claims that they establish the limits of a person's intellectual ability and that racial and ethnic groups possess fundamentally differing abilities. This discourse is widening and questions of the kind raised in this essay about standardized testing are being discussed. However, the discourse has had only a minimal impact on schools. It will only have greater impact if it broadens, and this can only happen if sufficient numbers of parents, teachers, and educational leaders begin to reconsider their own educational priorities. Each parent ought to consider, for a moment, the influence of standardized testing on their own and on their children's lives. Has it resulted in a better education? Has it led to greater learning opportunities or, have opportunities been closed off? For most of us, the assessment is a negative one. Afterall, half of the population falls below the norm, and, even for those who score above the norm, the im-

pact is likely negative given the kinds of intellectual operations
that are valued by the tests and how tests have come to influence
curriculum and instruction. We should insist that whatever takes
place in schools, including testing, be justified on general educational grounds. Do the tests represent what we value most for
our children and society? And, have they helped improve our
collective being? If not, then, they should either be done away
with or used in ways that will satisfy this standard. But, more
generally, we need to consider the impact of standardized testing
on the public world in which common interests have been
brushed aside casually in favor of accentuating comparatively
minor differences.

Excellence in those qualities that are most likely to revitalize the public world should be honored. We ought to care pas-
sionately that all young people be able to read with a high degree
of comprehension and be reasonably skilled in mathematics.
These operations do lend themselves to multiple choice testing.
They also should be able to interpret, analyze, and critique written works and oral presentations, and they should be able to
write decent sentences and essays. These operations require a
different kind of testing. But, how does one test for virtue? It
seems ludicrous to even make the attempt and yet, excellence in
this area should be valued above all others.

When testing does take place, the standard used to determine if a student has performed satisfactorily should not be a
national norm, but rather, the level of performance necessary to
be able to participate intelligently and fully in the public world.
Although difficult, it is entirely possible for such a standard to
be established and used, and teachers and parents ought to have
a hand in its creation. Anything lower, even if it reflects a national norm, is unacceptable.

As a people, we badly need to reconsider what counts as
excellence and how we are rewarding it. At this point in our
history, there appears to be no hope of doing away with standardized testing, nor, probably, should we. However, we must
exorcise our test score fetish, and begin to consider excellence
much more broadly than ever before and in relationship to the
values, understandings, and skills essential to a vital public
world.

5

Teachers and the Real World of Teaching

AN INTRODUCTION TO THE REAL WORLD

THE past year I worked with a group of twenty university students intent on obtaining a certificate that would entitle them to teach young people in grades seven through twelve. I came to know these people well, and to respect them. There was a mature woman from England who returned to school following the death of her husband and the graduation of her daughters from college. It was her turn to do something she wanted to do, and what she wanted was to teach. There was a very bright English and mathematics student who had a tendency to ask questions that made her instructors' palms sweat. She wanted to know there were good reasons behind what was done in class. And, there was a mild-mannered former athlete who had established himself as something of a legend on the football field for his aggressiveness and strength. Each was very different, but each was alike in his or her commitment to becoming a teacher.

During class breaks, I occasionally asked the students why they had decided to become teachers. For the most part there was a refreshing idealism in what they said. The football player had a job with an airline and ran a business on the side. Though doing well financially, he wanted something more out of life. He wanted a job that would "mean something" and teaching fit the requirement. A future biology teacher remarked that her own education was so poor that she felt compelled to try to do something to help others have a better experience than her own. Another simply loved literature and could not think of anything more wonderful to do than to share it. Yet another thought that young people were fascinating and funny and looked forward to being involved in their lives and problems. Not all their reasons were equally lofty, however. Some were uncertain if they actually would teach and, like practicing teachers, a few were motivated by very practical concerns such as the one mentioned by a math teacher in an interview: "I couldn't find . . . any other job except teaching that gave me [the summers off]."

These students, recently certified as teachers, will take their idealism and enthusiasm with them into the classroom. While there, however, they will begin to change; they will become teachers. What this means for many beginning teachers is that they must shed their idealism in favor of a pragmatic realism; they learn to do what they must in order to survive within the school factory. As one teacher put it, "Our field has more to do with survival than [with] professionalism."

In the process of surviving, many teachers come to be like Horace Smith, described in *Horace's Compromise*. Horace is a decent teacher. He knows his subject area, and he likes young people. But, Horace is cynical, something has happened to him over the years. When, for instance, a new idea comes along that promises to improve schooling he greets it with doubt, and those who champion such ideas are scorned: "They will find another panacea this time, probably the computer, and *of course* . . . it won't make much difference."[1] Horace long ago lost his enthusiasm for teaching. He is not in the least interested in doing anything differently than he has for many years. He does not hate his job; but he does not really like it either.

There are lots of Horaces teaching. Why is this so? How can it be that so many of the students I have come to care so much about will turn out this way in spite of all my good intentions? True, if my intentions, and that of the institution I serve, were fully honorable, my students would not be declared qualified to teach once they have completed their certificates. Rather, we would design programs that reflect a developmental view of teaching—teaching is less a state of *being* than of *becoming*—and provide for them a support system to nurture and to help them grow professionally, one that would follow them into their first years of teaching. But none of this happens. Instead, once they have their certificates in hand, we dump them and their idealism on the job market where they encounter what teachers are fond of calling the "real world."

There is no adequate definition of what is meant by the real world but every teacher knows what it is, and what it is not. Administrators are presumed to be only slightly familiar with this world, while professors know nothing of it. If I were to track my students down at the end of their first year of teaching I would find for many of them that, in the face of the real world, their enthusiasm will have waned and their idealism will have been tarnished.

Many veteran teachers snicker at the loss of rookie innocence and frequently take pleasure in having survived their first years without assistance. A first year teacher remarked that upon entering her school for the first time it was "like, here's your books, it's going to be a bad year." She felt "dumb asking questions" as though to ask for help was to admit weakness. The strong survive their encounter with the real world of teaching and the weak fall by the wayside unnoticed. All are changed by it.

There are many elements that make up the real world of teaching. Some have greater impact on teachers and on students than do others. Before mentioning what seem to me to be the more influential ones, a word should be said about the nature of their influence, origin, and importance. When we enter a hospital, a supermarket, or an elegant restaurant we act differently, and are treated differently. In part we know which kind of place we are in by the kinds of roles played by those who work within them. There is a busboy role, a physician role, a clerk role, and so on, each reflecting a set of standards and behaviors that are built into how work is thought of, organized, and institutionally supported. So it is with schools. There are teacher, student, and administrator roles that complement, reinforce, and strengthen one another and give schools their distinctive institutional flavor. So closely intertwined are these roles that in order to change one, all must be changed. If, for instance, the dominant role of student is one of passivity, as was mentioned in chapter two, then, one can be assured that the roles of teacher and administrator must be performed in such a way as to create this passive role.

Beginning teachers enter a school and, if they are to survive, must take upon them the essential features of the role of teacher. These are given, and the roles of student and administrator press their acceptance by vulnerable rookies. They are not, however, developed in isolation of the wider culture's values, nor are they immutable. Rather, institutional roles reflect and respond to larger societal priorities and adjust to them. Change of the teacher role is possible; it is also necessary, for without it there is little hope for educational improvement.

Recognition of this fact is the distinguishing characteristic of the second wave of school reform talk. The first wave, following publication of *A Nation At Risk* in 1983, paid little attention to teachers other than to point out their failings. The second wave, signaled by the publication of *A Nation Prepared: Teachers for the 21st Century* in 1986, brings with it an increased sensitivity to the plight of teachers and realization that they must be central players in any reform effort. The task before us is to reshape the role of the teacher and the institutional structure that maintains it, so that teachers will be encouraged to model the kinds of skills, attitudes, values, and understandings that we want developed in the young. If we want young people to be risk takers, then they must encounter teachers who are, themselves, risk takers; if we want young people who are concerned about and involved in political and economic issues, then they must encounter teachers who are similarly concerned and involved. For this to happen the teachers' world must be re-created.

THE REAL WORLD OF TEACHING IS . . .

The real world of teaching is low status. Physicians top our lists of the most respected professionals, while teachers hobble up near the rear, with only realtors and public officials trailing behind. It was not always so. When teaching was primarily the purview of aspiring ministers awaiting a calling to a church, teachers enjoyed considerable status, although they received very little pay.[2] The essence of teaching was character development and status came from knowing, serving, and doing good. To be a teacher was to represent higher values. In fact, teachers were often called to teaching. A few still are as a theater teacher's remarks suggest: teaching is "my gift . . . a god-given gift." Though some teachers still feel called to teaching, being called no longer brings with it status.

Many reasons have been given for the decline of the status of teaching. Some critics argue that when teaching became primarily a female profession, given our society's bias, all possibilities of attaining high status were removed. The feminization of teaching began early in America. In attempting to build the common schools of Massachusetts during the third decade of the nineteenth century, Horace Mann, for example, saw in women a cheap source of good, morally upstanding, labor. What are now traditional female occupations without exception are lower status and bring with them lower pay than male-dominated vocations. Accordingly, many talented women are leaving these areas for professions that are male-dominated. Unfortunately, the result is a further denigration of the occupations left behind.

It is also frequently argued that with the broad dissemination of the opportunity to gain an education, possession of a college degree no longer establishes status. Parents who are at least as well educated, and often better educated, than their children's teachers find it difficult to be impressed by them. And too, occupations that are dedicated to serving young people enjoy relatively low status in our society. In my more melancholy moods I wonder if as a society we really care much about our young people except when they are disruptive. Whatever the reasons, and these three seem to be good ones, teachers have little status.

The loss of status has been especially pronounced during the last twenty years. Longtime veterans speak nostalgically about what it was like when they first began teaching. A social studies teacher remarked, for example, that when he began teaching in 1956 "the students respected teachers. Today," he said, "they couldn't care less about the teachers. I think that's been basically because of the parents, too. Parents do not respect [teachers]. It is not a profession that's respected. [Their lack of respect is shown] in the wages they pay [us]." He longs for the good old days: "We had a lot more respect before." And, another teacher comments: "I guess [I have] felt for a long time that I'm a public servant . . . [a] slave and not well thought of. . . . I feel that in the conferences [I have with parents] . . . I can remember a parent conference last year that just totally crushed me because the woman just literally attacked me; [the] child was right. I almost wanted to go back to the days when the teacher was always right and the student never was right and the parents came in that way. I really did feel like that."

The average salary of teachers in the United States is about $24,000 which, at first glance, appears quite decent given a nine-month working year. But, this figure hides more than it reveals. When teacher salaries are projected on a twelve month basis, they fall short of the next lowest category, liberal arts graduates.[3] Moreover, teaching salaries top out at lower levels and much sooner than do the salaries of other college-educated workers. In my own state, which is slightly below the national average, a teacher starts at about $15,000 and, after twenty years of service, will receive about $27,000. It is a bitter pill for my students to swallow when they realize that their friends in engineering will have starting salaries that more than equal what veteran teachers are now receiving in most parts of the country. Over the past decade teacher salaries have declined substantially in real-dollar terms. From 1971 to 1981, for example, the decline was nearly 15 percent.[4]

One does not, as my teacher friends are fond of saying, go into teaching for the money. But, when the children of teachers qualify for subsidized school lunch and other forms of public assistance, and when, in order to make ends meet, excluding summer employment, over a third of all teachers find it necessary to hold part-time jobs, something is seriously amiss.[5] Such work, whether within or without the school, takes time and energy away from teaching. And it does something horrible to a teacher's self-esteem.

The importance of money and status to maintaining quality

schools is not readily apparent. Certainly many tremendously talented individuals will continue to seek personal fulfillment in teaching even if salary levels remain low. The issue, however, must be seen in comparison with teaching's ability to compete successfully with other professions for talented individuals. Schools are only as good as the teachers who teach within them. Without a substantial improvement in the status of teachers, we can expect to find fewer and fewer able persons aspiring to teach. Although public polls continue to show that a majority of Americans are willing to tax themselves at higher levels to improve salaries in the belief higher salaries will mean better education for their children, higher salaries alone, particularly the modest increases frequently mentioned, will do little to make teaching more attractive.[6]

The real world of teaching is hectic. It must become less so. Not long ago I spent part of a few days as a parent aid in my son's class. On one day, all I had to do was work with a small group of six youngsters to help them learn how to carry in addition. To help them learn this complex concept, we had different colored beans representing ones and tens that we moved around a sheet of paper divided into ones and tens columns. I would give a problem, add 29 and 43, for instance, and the students would then count out the appropriate number of tens and ones and give me the answer. The students liked this exercise with "manipulatives" as did I. Soon, however, I became a bit frustrated. Part way through the lesson, one boy had to leave for "resource." Resource is a place where kids who need special attention of many different kinds go for brief periods of instruction during the day. All day long they are coming and going, making it very difficult in some classrooms to maintain continuity of learning. Shortly after this boy left, another arrived. There are many such students in classes now. Some require a tremendous amount of special attention. A few would have been placed in separate classrooms not long ago, but, under the influence of recent federal legislation requiring that young people be placed in the least restrictive educational environments they can reasonably handle, they are now in regular classrooms and teachers must deal with them. This is a good idea, but it increases the difficulty of teaching. Some of the young people did the problems very rapidly while others, for a variety of reasons, trailed along behind. Some were too interested in goofing off to move along very quickly. Others seemed to not understand what we were doing and with these I spent additional time. All wanted my attention and I gave it. But imagine, for a moment, what it is like to spend from 8:15 A.M. until 2:30 P.M. every day with not six, but twenty-seven seven and eight year-olds all needing help!

Each hour of every day, teachers in elementary schools are called upon to make two hundred or more decisions.[7] Secondary teachers, who meet hour after hour with a new class of as many as thirty-five students, face a similar challenge. There is simply no way for teachers to respond enthusiastically or, for that matter, to respond fully to all the demands placed upon them. No matter how furiously and efficiently they work, there is always something that is undone: a child who needs, but does not get, a particular book; a hallway that goes unpatrolled; a kind word that goes unsaid. It is little wonder that teaching is only slightly less stressful than working as an air traffic controller.

The pace of work is increased by the burden of paperwork, which worsens every year in response to district demands for accountability. But even without accountability pressures, conscientious teachers rarely find themselves having sufficient time to interact with students because of the need to get through all the paperwork. Attendance must be taken, tardies marked, notes written to parents, instructional objectives and lesson plans written, materials ordered, tests and assignments written, and papers graded and recorded.

To do all that is required of them, most teachers have more than a 40-hour workweek. Let us say an English teacher decides that every other week her students will write a short, two-page, paper. In high schools, teaching loads of 150 students or more are very common. To lighten the burden, only 75 students will be writing a paper each week. Let us imagine that this teacher is an especially efficient one and can read each paper and comment on it in five minutes. Five times 75 gives us 375 minutes. In effect, by giving this small assignment, our teacher friend can expect to have a little over an hour's worth of grading to do every night, or over six hours one evening. Imagine the impact on a teacher's time if the assignment is a term paper! As one teacher put it: "Sometimes I'm not a human being . . . I . . . punch the clock and go home [carrying] 40 notebooks . . . Give me one more day!" When paperwork arising from the concern for accountability is added, it is little wonder that teachers feel, as one young science teacher put it, "overwhelmed by paperwork."

Accountability increases a teacher's work load in a variety of ways. In many districts teachers must turn in daily lesson plans, and do a myriad of little things to prove they are doing their jobs. An example comes to mind. During a junior high school faculty meeting I attended, the principal announced that the district was getting very concerned about the possibility of being sued by a disgruntled parent. In order to prepare for this remote possibility, all teachers would be required to mark in their roll books the topics covered each day in class. To make certain the teachers complied, he announced he would be calling in the roll books of selected groups of faculty members. The response to this announcement was hardly enthusiastic. Some teachers asked if their lesson plans would suffice; they would not, and they were not told why. Making good on his threat, the next week the principal called in the roll books of a group of seventh grade teachers who were given a day's notice. The evening before the day of reckoning was spent by these teachers reworking their roll books.

Yet another example comes to mind. Presumably to improve the quality of instruction in our schools many states are now funding career ladders. To receive a career ladder, a teacher must make a case that he or she is an excellent teacher and deserving of more pay than less able teachers or, in many locations, make a proposal for a project that will improve the school program in some way. The former plan is supposed to reward high quality teaching, while the later actually represents a means for providing part-time but school-related employment for teachers. To prove they are outstanding, teachers must put together a dossier, what teachers in one school district call a "brag book." A brag book takes an incredible amount of time to put together — twenty to thirty hours — and is composed of virtually everything and anything a teacher can think of that will convince a superior that they deserve the money. In some schools, brag books are standing jokes, "One junior high school teacher says teachers at his school have quipped that they'll package their peers in an impressive dossier for a $50 fee."[8] Time spent in these ways does little to enhance the quality of a teacher's professional life. Indeed, by putting teachers in competition with one another for limited funds and taking time away from other activities, it does much to denigrate it.

The real world of teaching is controlled. Schools are organized bureaucratically and hierarchically. At the top of the pyramid are adminstrators and at the bottom are students. Somewhere in the middle are teachers who sometimes get the feeling they share the bottom rung. The lack of teachers' control over their professional lives shows up in a multitude of ways. One teacher, in disgust, commented that she had virtually no say over the curriculum she was to teach. "It was done at the board level, strictly at the board level . . . with absolutely no input from . . . teachers. . . . We're down on the rock bottom with the kids where we see it and they're [those who make the curriculum] up sitting on their thrones making these decisions. There was no input. There was no committee. There was nothing. . . . The first day that we came back [following summer break] they handed us an outline. . . . They just handed it to us!"

A teacher's day is controlled in other ways as well; they have little say over the classes they will teach, or over the students with whom they will interact. Few are involved in deciding which textbooks will be used. They are told when to eat lunch, and, because of the importance of testing, the range of instructional options before them is severely restricted.

Sadly, in many locations teacher associations have done little to improve the situation. More and more, contracts read like lists of rules that bind more than they liberate. The union itself represents a mighty bureaucracy. When problems arise, teachers pass them along to the building association representative, who in turn passes them along. Eventually, a general solution will be negotiated if the problem is of sufficient importance to receive such attention. The process is typically a very slow one that grinds on while problems simmer. What is important for teachers is that face-to-face problem solving is replaced by a system that produces binding solutions that may or may not speak sensitively to the context that initially produced the complaint. Once a solution is agreed upon, all are held to it. Although there are very good reasons for organizing, particularly to assure a measure of justice in the workplace, the emphasis on prescribing behavior through establishing rules and regulations for everything, rather than stressing principles of behavior and a code of ethics similar in spirit to the Hippocratic Oath, retards development of professionalism. A math teacher nicely sums up the result of the collusion between the association and the real world of teaching: "I'm treated as though I'm some sort of a lacky . . . you have to do this, you have to do that, you have to do the other thing. You're really constrained in your life. You're stuck."

The real world of teaching is standardized. Teachers are treated as interchangeable parts in a mighty system of public education; one math teacher is presumed to be like any other. And, as noted in chapter two, there is a surprising uniformity in how teachers teach. Having to deal with large numbers of students and generally with inadequate materials encourages dependence on lecturing. Most teachers, I suspect, would like to take some instructional risks but do not see how it is possible to do anything other than what they do. The fear of losing control of students further discourages risk taking as does the importance of standardized test scores. There are, however, other pressures that encourage teacher standardization that bear mentioning.

Throughout the country Americans are demanding that teachers be evaluated. Teacher evaluation is not, inherently, a bad idea. But, our national fascination with systems, our distrust of teachers and others charged with serving our interests, and our demand for efficiency of a narrow kind, have led to the adoption of an approach to teacher evaluation that is likely to have precisely the opposite of the desired effects.

Sixty percent of us want teacher competency tests of some kind to be administered to make certain we are getting high quality teachers.[9] Such tests, like the widely used National Teachers Examination produced by ETS, have all the problems of standardized testing mentioned in chapter four and more. At base, they have no connection whatsoever with the ability to teach, and they encourage the tendency to define excellence in terms of the ability to meet minimum standards.[10]

Given our biases, it is not surprising that many of the attempts to evaluate teachers based upon actual job performance have strengthened systemwide tendencies toward standardization, and made the job less enjoyable and attractive. Many teachers resent being evaluated, and for good reason; typically evaluation is done for punitive reasons. "It is just a snooper thing. It creates those feelings, well, 'I'm nervous, I better look [good] today.' That's not teaching—I could always look good when people come into my room when I want to. . . . I know what they look for [but] I want something different."

But, even when evaluation is not "a snooper thing" and is done on a sustained basis, its result may be professionally debilitating. The Florida Performance Measurement System is a good example. The explicit aim of the system is to identify meritorious teachers. Further, those who champion this system believe that it "holds promise of significant and dramatic improvement in classroom practice, substantive change in both preservice and inservice teacher education, and refinement and extension of knowledge about teaching practice."[11] Its implicit aim, however, is to control teacher behavior. To do so, "one hundred and twenty-one specific teacher behaviors that have been shown through research to be directly related to increased student achievement (read test scores) and improved classroom conduct" were identified.[12] Armed with a checklist, observers go into classrooms and check off which behaviors are present. Meritorious teachers will demonstrate all the appropriate behaviors. The assumption is that researchers have definitively established what effective teacher behaviors are, and that these behaviors are identical across school contexts; "The underlying premise is that there is a single set of teaching behaviors that constitutes effective teaching over all subject areas and grade levels."[13] Teaching inner-city black students English, in this view, is precisely like teaching AP (advanced placement) calculus classes to suburban, upper middle-class, whites. This is hardly the case.

The conclusions provided by research are always and everywhere tentative and conditional; research provides generalizations, but teachers work with specific children, in particular classrooms, and schools. The appropriate application of generalizations requires intelligence and sensitivity on the part of teachers. They must be able to recognize, based upon intimate knowledge of their students, of themselves, and of the school within which they work, when a generalization does not hold true. There are, therefore, no hard and fast rules of good teaching; research cannot tell a teacher what to do, it can, however, inform a teacher's judgement. It does in fact make a difference where one teaches, what one teaches, and to whom. And it makes a great deal of difference what the purposes of instruction are, as noted in chapter four. We would expect, and hope, that teachers will be different, and that they will use the generalizations of research wisely. Yet, many of the evaluation schemes in use press teachers to be alike with the result that creative people are driven out of teaching and performance is leveled.

The real world of teaching is contradictory. When teachers begin talking with one another about what is expected of them by administrators, parents, and young people, and what they expect of themselves frustration soon follows. One teacher remarked, "You talk to the parents and you realize, 'okay, I'm the one who's supposed to do everything.' . . . You're trying to do all these things to sort of meet everybody's needs and then, you sort of have the dominant feeling of society that you're a piece of shit." Another teacher commented, that "last year [the administration] made two advanced classes [by pulling] out all of the kids [who did not have problems] but left in all of those that had reading disabilities and learning problems. I had no one in my classes to help the [other] kids be motivated, [no] stronger and better learners." To provide what was presumed to be a better education for some, others were put into a situation that was harmful to them; one group wins, the others lose.

Grades too, are a source of constant frustration: should a teacher grade on ability? On effort? On what? If students are graded primarily on ability, less able students get discouraged. But, if they are graded on effort, able students may actually receive grades lower than their less able peers. If this happens, as it often does, teachers are giving a message to the public that they care little about standards when the truth is, they are using standards, just different ones. No matter how teachers resolve the dilemma, they, and some students, lose. "There was no way I could rationalize passing them," an English teacher remarked after going to extraordinary measures to help a small group of students having difficulty in her class. She realized she was neglecting the other students and, in dismay, concluded, "you have an obligation to . . . the other 82 percent . . . as well."

The real world of teaching is lonely. Teachers spend very little of their day with adults. Secondary education teachers typically have five minutes between periods and a short, perhaps twenty minute lunch during which, "if you want to talk to people . . . you might as well not eat." Elementary school teachers might see another teacher for a few moments while supervising recess, and perhaps for a brief period of time during lunch, but, here too, they enjoy very little adult interaction. It is little wonder that teachers of very young children sound like children themselves in their conversation with other adults. The lack of adult interaction is not the only problem. When teachers do meet with other teachers, typically the conversation is about technical-managerial matters, such as scheduling or how to put in a book order. There is little time to talk about personal matters, and, even when there is sufficient time, the need to, as one teacher put it, "appear expert," mitigates against sharing problems and concerns. Teachers are isolated by the organization of the school day and the structure of the school building. They are also isolated by the choices they make. They may not like the loneliness of teaching, but they find utility in their isolation within the building. Of this, more will be said later.

The real world of teaching is low status, hectic, controlled, standardized, contradictory, and lonely, and it is increasingly unattractive as an occupational choice, especially to talented young people. For teaching to become more attractive, teaching, itself, must be changed. Our situation is serious, in some respects desperate. Within a very few years a substantial percentage of teachers now teaching will be retiring. Experienced teachers are leaving in droves. For example, in a recent Louis Harris poll, 19 percent of the teachers surveyed, who had less than five years of teaching, said they will be quitting; 29 percent

of those with five to nine years of experience, 25 percent of
those with ten to nineteen years on the job, and 30 percent of
those with twenty or more years of experience report they are
likely to leave teaching within the next five years.[14] In total, one
half of all teachers quit within the first seven years. Moreover,
we are facing significant teacher shortages in mathematics,
chemistry, physics, English, and several other areas. Soon, there
will be a huge general shortage of teachers. While we consider
the question of how we will meet this shortage, and the type of
person we would like to see enter teaching, we must consider
carefully what it is we are offering to attract talented people to
teaching and to keep good teachers on the job.

At present, there is too little to commend teaching. As one
teacher put it, "If you enjoy . . . public contumely, contempt,
and derision, topped by a heavy helping of ignorant argument,
then you ought to become a public school teacher. If you have a
masochistic streak, then you ought to become a public school
teacher. But if you have self-respect, if you love your subject,
and know it as the public does not, then go another way because
this career road will only cause you grief."[15] Dissatisfaction
within the teaching ranks is rapidly increasing. One-third of all
teachers would quit teaching now if another job came along
with a comparable salary. Only 40 percent of all teachers are
very satisfied with their jobs compared to 52 percent of the
working public. The best qualified, better educated teachers, are
the most dissatisfied.[16] Less than half of the current teaching
force plans to teach until retirement. It is only as the role of
teacher is changed, that teaching will become an attractive career option.

TEACHER SURVIVAL STRATEGIES

Teachers respond to the conditions of the real world of
teaching in a variety of ways. Some become like Horace Smith,
others quietly pack their bags and leave teaching believing, as
one teacher remarked, that "nobody should stay in teaching
long." Those who do endure, including Horace, develop a va-

riety of survival strategies that, when effectively employed, absorb and soften the blows of the real world of teaching. Ironically, the strategies make the intolerable tolerable and thereby impede efforts to substantially alter the teacher role.

The strategies reflect a set of values and attitudes, a mindedness, that develops in teachers in response to the situation within which they find themselves. These include presentism, an all pervasive concern with classroom matters to the exclusion of larger educational issues; individualism, a desire to be left alone and to work alone; and conservatism, an unwillingness to change. Taken together, presentism, individualism, and conservatism justify, to the minds of many teachers, a variety of teacher strategies that appear on the surface to be contrary to institutional expectations, just as they make it possible for the essential features of the public school system to continue. We humans are remarkably adaptive, unfortunately, our ability to survive sometimes prevents us from working to alter the conditions that demand adaptation of us. In effect we become, to use Erich Fromm's language, comfortable in the chains of our illusion; we become incapable of imagining the world not as it is.

There is tremendous utility for teachers in holding to the values of presentism, individualism, and conservatism. Presentism allows teachers to prioritize demands and to resolve some contradictions. Any request that takes time away from students will be dismissed out of hand as inconsistent with what a good teacher ought to be doing. Attention is diverted away from considering the aims of education, where controversy abounds, while careful consideration is given to means. Similarly, when expectations are contradictory a teacher will resolve them in some fashion behind the privacy of the classroom door where they are protected from the roving eye of ever-watchful critics. It is for this reason that teachers value their isolation. Some teachers make no bones about it. As one teacher put it, "I like my isolation."

Individualism complements teacher isolation. By working independently of others, teachers can take some instructional risks without fear of raising eyebrows. They might even break some rules, safe in the knowledge that no one will ever know—

administrators cannot possibly control all that happens in schools, let alone in classrooms, and so most teachers likely engage in occasional contrary action. One teacher remarked, for example, that she had a lot of control over the curriculum, although no one was aware of it and she was not supposed to have it: "I shouldn't [have control] because I'm supposed to teach what's on the standardized tests and all that stuff. I ignore that. I really do. . . . I don't like the isolation but I like the independence. . . . I'm in my own classroom and I can do whatever I want." Other teachers use their isolation in similar ways, linking it closely to feelings of autonomy.

Conservatism also has a payoff. For the most part teachers stick to the tried-and-true methods when teaching. They take few risks, at least ones that will call attention to them. By taking few risks they protect themselves from adverse feedback. I have to "draw the line because I feel the feedback I would get from the community-at-large would not be good for me. . . . Not that they would disapprove necessarily [of what I do], but they would feel that's not my job as an educator. . . . For instance, I am personally really involved in Greenpeace and stuff like that. I feel very strongly [about environmental issues]. I would love to do something with that [but] I don't feel that society considers that my job. So, I don't do it." Furthermore, conservatism is a source of teacher power of a negative kind. Administrators see teachers as major impediments to school change. Their goal is to obtain teachers' compliance to administrator initiated innovations. By refusing to go along, or by going along half-heartedly, teachers are able to exercise a measure of control over the workplace, avoid false starts and wasted energy, and extract from administrators some concessions.

Presentism, individualism, and conservatism are, in a sense, themselves, strategies for institutional survival. They reflect an ideology and psychology of teaching within American public schools. From them flow specific means for manipulating portions of the environment to make it more tolerable and more enjoyable. Three categories of action emerge from my observations of classrooms, reflecting what others do within massive and complex bureaucracies: teachers ignore, minimally comply, and quietly subvert superior's demands, and they do so, often fully aware of their actions. Examples of each response easily come to mind.

Teachers engage in a large number of noninstructional duties throughout the school year. Sponsors must be found for the debate, dance, Key, and a variety of other clubs. Someone must agree to work with the student government. Someone must patrol the halls and monitor detention. The list is endless. In some schools, where the expectation is that every teacher will participate in such activities, teachers sign up at the beginning of the year. In one such school, one teacher quietly neglected to sign up wondering if "they actually went through the list." He was caught by a secretary and at that point "had to sign up." But if he had been successful, he would have enjoyed a little more time for activities he valued. In another area, this same teacher had successfully lightened his paperwork load by not bothering to take roll every class period, as was required by the school, opting instead to only take it first period as required by the state.

Minimal compliance is a survival strategy widely employed by teachers. Throughout the nation teachers are required to turn in lesson plans to administrators. The reasons for doing so are not always clear, but occasionally plans are reviewed. Teachers quickly learn from other teachers what will minimally satisfy the principal and either write down or up to that standard.

Examples of teacher subversion of administrative demands are more difficult to identify. There is much greater risk involved in being discovered and so, teachers become especially secretive. Teachers who get caught might receive letters of reprimand that may, at some future point, come back to haunt them. The more secure route is to minimally comply, and then pass along a grievance to the professional association. Occasionally, however, if enough time is spent with a teacher in a classroom, an event will come along that prompts a teacher to engage in subversion.

When I was a boy, every student had to attend a homeroom class. In some school districts the modern version of homeroom is Teacher Advisory (TA). Every week for one full period a group of students and a teacher get together to plan schedules, discuss careers, and talk about values, what one teacher, who resented having time taken away from academics, called "self-concept garbage." The district put together a TA curriculum guide that contained some suggestions for use of the time. Teachers were expected to have lesson plans for each session but very few did. Independently, a large portion of the faculty decided they would not spend their time in this way. The teacher I observed sometimes ran regular class periods believing the time better spent. And, occasionally, he and a colleague combined their classes and ran films that seemed to them of some interest and importance. They would not, and did not formally plan for TA. As it turns out, so many teachers were quietly subverting the program it got back to the principal who demanded that each teacher turn in plans several weeks ahead for their TA periods. To this end, the principal set aside time in a faculty meeting for groups of teachers to work on their plans. At this point, the teachers' strategy shifted from one of quiet subversion, to minimal compliance. Each group of teachers threw together plans they thought would minimally satisfy the principal. But, there was no assurance that they would follow their plans once inside the classroom. Wisely, the principal did not begin observing TA classes.

The teachers' objection to TA was not only that it took up valuable instructional time, but also that it added yet another preparation period to their already busy schedules and that the content was boring to students and trivial when treated in isolation of other topics. Ultimately, what motivated the objections was not teacher laziness, but the belief that TA was not educationally defensible.

The real world of teaching shapes how teachers understand their work, and how they perform in the classroom. It does not, however, fully determine what they think or how they act; there is always some tension between a teacher's values and beliefs about education and the institution's. When what the teacher values and what the institution values run into conflict, as they often do, the teacher will, whenever possible, try to preserve his or her own values. This is important because, what teachers value, more than anything else, are students and student learning. Unfortunately, this cannot be said of schooling as it is institutionalized. "Sometimes," a teacher remarked, "I really feel like I'm . . . teaching something and they're [the students] really learning and . . . responding and asking questions — and I'm not babysitting, not taking someone out in the hall, and I'm not sitting and adding points, and all those little cruddy things that you have to do — I really feel like the kids are involved and they're all with me, it just feels *so* good. It doesn't happen very often. . . . We don't get enough of those experiences. We're so bogged down with . . . all the things we have to do all the time." Another teacher commented that "when I actually feel like I'm teaching and I'm getting through to somebody it's exciting. It is really neat to me. I really enjoy it. . . . I really, really, enjoy that, but I get to do that so seldom. . . . I don't get to teach very often." This teacher further commented that, to her, "it seems almost like the schools, in general, are structured for making you . . . feel like a failure."

As I have noted, teachers quietly subvert the real world of teaching while acting in ways that preserve it. They do not like it this way, but that is the way it is. In isolation they each come to a compromised truce, or they leave teaching. However, quality education cannot be had when often it is dependent upon the willingness of teachers to subvert rules. What is necessary is to rework the role of teacher and the institutional arrangements that sustain it.

There currently is considerable disagreement about how to go about improving schools. Not surprisingly, many proposals assume that teachers are the central educational problem. Operating on this assumption, various proposals have been presented that aim at controlling teachers to make certain they do as they should. The Florida evaluation scheme reflects this point of view. Others, who share this assumption, are less obvious. Donna Kerr, for example, argues that hope lies in training and hiring "doctors of teaching" who, as experts in charge of twenty or so teachers, will somehow get teachers to behave as they should.[17] Too little attention has been given to why teachers do what they do.

What amazes me is how many fine teachers there are, given the work conditions they face. Sadly, such teachers exist almost despite of the system within which they serve. The system ought to help teachers to be models of intellectual curiosity, commitment, compassion, and courage; instead, it rewards a survivalist mentality, and frustrates and demoralizes many of them. They deserve better, and so do our young people.

When considering some of the changes that will help good teachers become better teachers, we should be guided in our efforts by a few watchwords: contrary to the reform movements of the past century, which have led to greater and greater centralization (since 1960 we have reduced the number of school districts from 40,000 to 16,000 while increasing the number of administrators by 83 percent), we ought to decentralize. Small and simple is better than large and complex. And personal is always and everywhere better than impersonal. Programs ought not ever stand between people. When materials are doing the bulk of the teaching, when students spend most of their time sitting at desks, heads bent over, interacting with worksheets, or when they must sit passively listening, education suffers. It also suffers when teachers simply do not have the time to interact with students. Finally, and again contrary to the reform movements of the past century in which specialization has ruled and experts have dominated, we ought to flatten and dissemble bureaucracies and hierarchies. Teachers are experts in education and they ought to enjoy the work conditions necessary to function professionally. It is only when teachers have the autonomy and responsibility enjoyed by other professionals that it is reasonable to hold them accountable for their work. Otherwise, someone else up the hierarchy ought to be held accountable. Minimally, those who are to live and work within schools — teachers and students — ought to have a hand in determining the kind of life that will be lived there.

One step in the right direction is to break up our large schools. A graduating class of one hundred is large enough to maintain a respectable academic program. A high school of four hundred, grades nine through twelve, is manageable and educationally sensible. There is no secret to establishing such schools. Since the 1960s virtually every school district in the United States has some school-within-a-school program operating. Justification for such programs frequently includes statements about the need to make education more personal for those who were having difficulties with the system. Similarly, Advanced Placement students have had this benefit by virtue of being tracked into higher level courses that they share throughout the day. We should extend that logic. Young people and their teachers ought to be allowed to become part of small learning communities even within large schools.

Within a small learning community, education becomes a more likely outcome than it is currently. But smallness alone will not solve our problems. It is a necessary but not sufficient condition. The work of teachers must be simplified. At a minimum they need to be relieved of most, if not all, of their noninstructional duties (currently between 10 percent and 50 percent of a teacher's time is spent in this way). It is especially important that the burden of paperwork, which threatens to bury teachers, be lightened. If we want teachers to act like professionals, then we ought to treat them as professionals. To accomplish this end, teachers will need help in the classroom but such help need not be prohibitively expensive. The huge pool of senior citizens we have in America is one logical place to look for help. College students and older public school students should also be involved.

The work of teachers must be personalized; diversity should be cherished, not merely tolerated. Accomplishing this requires a much better use of talent than is currently the practice. Better schools will come when teachers have the opportunity to engage, primarily, in activities they enjoy and have a reasonable possibility of doing well. The implication is that not all teachers ought to engage in precisely the same activities. Not all need to be good lecturers, skilled in small group discussion, or effective coaches. The flexibility allowed by a small school-within-a-school makes it possible to better utilize talent. In order to do so, however, we must get away from notions that every teacher must have the same number of students and begin thinking creatively about ways to internally reallocate resources. If, for example, every student must obtain a given body of knowledge and lecture is the way to do it, why not give one lecture to everyone followed by discussion groups to clear up confusion and to explore ideas more fully? The current practice is to give the same lecture several times to different classes which makes little sense at all. To this end teacher preparation should entail models that will prepare teachers for different settings: large, medium, and small groups.

Finally, those within a learning community must be given the right and responsibility for establishing instructional programs and rules of governance. In doing so, local communities, the academy, and the claims of a democracy on education must each be satisfied. Just as the local community may press for provincialism, the claims of the academy and of democracy press the interests of the wider human community. It is within the school that these interests need to be brought together; the school is and ought to be a place in constant tension and conflict without which education is, once again, an impossibility.

When combined with appropriate salary increases these changes, modest as they are, would go far toward altering the teacher role. They are all well within our grasp. Individual school faculties and administrators even now could begin moving to embrace them. There are, however, some obstacles in the way of reform, not the least of which is the set of values — presentism, individualism, and conservatism — teachers have developed while learning to cope with the conditions of teaching. At times, teachers are their own worst enemies. Although resilient, these values can be weakened; few, if any, teachers actually like them. When their presence is recognized, teachers only hold to them primarily because they see no reasonable alternatives. When other possibilities arise, those teachers who have not already done so, will gradually shed the psychological and ideological residue of the real world of teaching that limits their educational vision and prevents them from being more actively involved in shaping their own professional destinies.

6

School Knowledge
and Human Experience

When thinking about school reform comparatively little attention has been given to the nature of school knowledge (knowledge derived from course content) or to the nature of the encounters young people have with it. For the most part educators have been too busy responding to critics by trying to cram more "solids" or substantive courses—assuming that this implies academic courses that are more rigorous—into young peoples' programs, to be troubled by such questions. However, requiring more of something does not make sense unless what is required is genuinely educative. More attention needs to be paid to the substantive nature of the courses as they are, and as they should be.

The way in which school content is commonly spoken of reveals how it is understood. Young people take courses just as they would take a can of Campbell's soup from the grocer's shelf. Once they have finished it, they have "had physics" or they have "had American history." Little is done to integrate the various courses or the knowledge derived from them. This creates a fragmented view of knowledge in which bits and pieces of content are presumably deposited into young peoples' heads for later retrieval. The question is then, what do these human

---

An earlier version of this essay first appeared in the *Educational Forum*. 51 (1987).

cans contain, and should anyone bother to consume what is in them?

To answer this two-part question it is necessary to scrutinize textbooks and textbook publishing; we must examine the kinds of experiences young people have with content and how it is made available to them. As indicated here, content is really refined and organized human experience. When considering content, the consumption metaphor is actually a good starting point. The task for educators is to create an environment that facilitates the internalization of knowledge by the student so that it becomes part of each individual's experience, and as such, useful for solving problems and enriching life. Internalization brings with it increased personal power, and the potential for gaining greater control over life. Comprehension of the prior experience of the human race (knowledge) and an understanding of the use of the tools of inquiry (the refined modes of thinking) that characterize the disciplines are essential to achieving this end. Without question, if a young person is to become a fully participating member of society, then school content, the organized experience of others, must be internalized. Without it, the individual is dependent and extremely vulnerable to the whims of others and to the press of incomprehensible events. Moreover, internalizing this experience is essential to personal fulfillment.

TEXTBOOKS AND COURSE CONTENT

In American classrooms, the quality and often the quantity of the content made available to students depends upon how good, or how bad the textbooks are. With textbooks, especially in elementary schools, come sample tests, worksheets, and suggested activities that, taken together, form entire programs that define content and dominate instruction. As former students we are all too familiar with the power of the textbook, and its accompanying worksheets, to shape learning. One estimate is that 75 percent of a student's classroom time and 90 percent of homework time is spent with textbook materials.[1]

Market considerations have a profound influence on the materials that eventually end up in the hands of students. Driven by the profit motive, textbook publishers are much more interested in making a sale than in producing a product that is academically and ethically responsible; they do whatever it takes to sell their materials. To this end, they engage in a kind of self-censorship based upon their worst fears of offending potential customers.[2] For example, controversial issues or topics are washed out for fear of alienating a potential buyer.

To help authors avoid offending, major publishers routinely distribute "a list of guidelines on topics to avoid." The list of dangerous topics is seemingly endless and includes "political figures in American history over whom controversy still exists: F.D.R., Nixon and Agnew, for example; living people who might possibly become infamous; topics that would undermine legitimate authority — the family, the government and its branches, teachers, police and so forth; poems and stories written by known or suspected dissidents."[3] Phyllis Schlafly helps identify more specifically some of these threatening topics. In her view, schools should avoid dealing with "parental conflict, sex, death, drugs, murder, suicide, mental illness, poverty, despair and anger."[4] Other taboo topics include "references that put the free enterprise system in a bad light; evolution, magic, fortune-telling, . . . arcades, video games, skateboarding, religious holidays, and censored books."[5] One wonders, how it is even possible to teach history or any of the social sciences let alone English literature given this point of view?

When a controversial topic somehow slips past censors, publishers have proven themselves remarkably responsive to critics — damn the quality of the content. Hoping to make the *American Heritage Dictionary* more palatable, for example, the representatives of the publisher, Houghton Mifflin, offered to delete offensive words.[6] Not many controversial items get past the censors and into print; even the classics are not excused from censorship. *Romeo and Juliet* is 400 words shorter than Shakespeare intended in the Scott, Foresman and Company anthology, *Arrangement in Literature*. There was just too much "sexually explicit material" in the play.[7]

Content is also flattened by state procedures for textbook

adoption. In nearly half the states, textbook adoption is centralized, residing in the hands of small, often highly politicized committees. If a state is highly centralized in its adoption procedure and represents a large market, it can exercise considerable influence over the content of textbooks for the entire nation. Publishers do not want to offend Texans, for example, who annually account for about six percent of the total textbook market. Until 1984 science textbooks read in the classrooms of Texas were required to present evolution as only one of several theories on how life began, an editorial decision that had a ripple effect on texts nationwide. It was only after a concerted effort on the part of such groups as The Texas Council for Science Education that the state school board reversed its "anti-science textbook policy" which had "so intimidated science textbook publishers that the topic of evolution [had] been reduced almost to nothing in most biology and geology textbooks."[8]

The anti-science policy arose in part because of political pressure from the far right, especially from Mel and Norma Gabler's Educational Research Analysts which publishes reviews of textbooks. Centralization of the textbook decision-making process, along with the responsiveness of the state textbook adoption committee to pressure, apparently allowed the Gablers to get what they wanted. The Gablers are quite clear about what is at stake in arguments over textbook content: "Textbooks mold nations because they determine how a nation votes, what it becomes, and where it goes." And further, "Until textbooks are changed, there is no possibility that crime, abortion, or VD rates will decrease."[9] In their view, the battle over textbook content is a battle over the kind of America we will have.

The vision they have of human rights and of citizenship obligations is quite clear, and strikingly undemocratic. They fear knowledge, widely disseminated, and are distrustful of human nature. In the name of protecting children they seek conformity and obedience, "leaving students to make up their own minds about things just isn't fair to our children."[10] They hope to eliminate discussion of controversial issues and, ignoring the role of interpretation in knowledge production, believe only facts are worthy school content; there is a right answer to every question deserving consideration in our schools. As Mrs. Gabler put it,

"A concept will never do anyone as much good as a fact" — and, of course, evolution is not a fact.[11]

The standards used to guide adoption decisions also often result in a weakening of content. Once again, in Texas any citizen can challenge a specific textbook being considered for adoption by filing a "Bill of Particulars" six weeks before the public hearing which allows publishers time to respond to charges in writing.[12] In mid-August publishers and protestors meet to give public testimony before the State Textbook Committee. At this meeting only publishers are allowed to speak in defense of a text; citizens may criticize, but they cannot praise. Following this meeting the State Textbook Committee recommends to the commissioner of education no more than five books per subject, and no fewer than two. The commissioner, in turn, applies his own standards and may require textbook publishers to make changes prior to passing along a recommendation to the State Board of Education. Without satisfying the commissioner a text is doomed. Prior to final adoption the State Board of Education conducts its own hearings, which may result in approval or further demands for revision. At each review point the wise publisher works hard to avoid offense, the most essential criterion for adoption.

It is little wonder that most of the textbooks our children read are bland and uninteresting. Our children read thoroughly disinfected literature and history in school. But, there is something else that is just as destructive to young people as their being forced to consume intellectual gruel. Textbooks are supposed to present the truth. And what is the truth they present, particularly to working- and middle-class children? The content force-fed to children is sanitized, removed from the struggle with ignorance that lies behind it; knowledge is finished, completed, in the hands of mysterious experts who produce facts that are well beyond the influence of ordinary people. Remote, unknown, others make history; history is not made by young people or by their parents. They are spectators, isolated on the sidelines while others interpret and shape their cultural heritage. It is also pasteurized and homogenized. The world, according to many textbooks, is neatly divided into good and bad people.

A result is that the disciplines of knowledge suffer when

their life is flushed out. The tools that are used to create and define knowledge within all the disciplines (physics, chemistry, or literary criticism for example) are reduced to rules that should govern knowledge acquisition rather than promoted as means of thinking, fundamental and effective means for finding and testing meaning. I recall in my own school experience having to memorize precisely the steps of the scientific method (somehow the number of steps varied depending on the teacher) without ever understanding the connection between what I was to learn and science. The reason why I failed to make the link was, I believe, that there was not a link to be made. School content had nothing to do with learning how to think systematically; thinking is unnecessary when the aim of schooling is to memorize the facts.

What many young people are taught, implicitly and explicitly, about the nature of knowledge is a lie. Education, as it is, denies the struggle with ignorance, confusion, and prejudice (the kind described in *The Double Helix)* that one must face to obtain knowledge. This denial belittles the experience of gaining knowledge; it encourages students to believe that school subject matter has nothing to do with the struggle to understand. Nor are students allowed to see that embedded in school subject matter, all content, is a variety of human interests; hidden behind the serene scenes presented in a glossy-covered textbook is a struggle between conflicting interests to define the public and private spheres. Instead, young people are taught that nothing, really, is at stake: content is value free. Moreover, the lie requires that teachers commit phoney attempts to make subject matter relevant. The result is that very few young people ever have the opportunity to actively and fully encounter the accumulated experience of the human race which is necessary if it is to connect with individual life experience.

ACCESSIBILITY TO KNOWLEDGE

How textbooks and other instructional materials are made available by teachers to students also has a profound impact on school content. We are beginning to discover, sadly, that one of the key variables is social class. School content is something quite different for working-, middle-, and upper-class kids. Lurking behind those identically labeled credits in mathematics or history that students accumulate toward graduation, for instance, are very different encounters with different kinds of content. One study, for example, compared fifth grade classes in five elementary schools; two classified as working-class, one as middle-class, one as affluent professional, and one as executive elite based upon income, occupation, and a variety of other social characteristics.[13]

The vast majority of our young people attend either working- or middle-class schools. In comparison, very few attend either the affluent professional or the executive elite type schools. Within working class schools the researcher found that content was composed of rules and facts. Emphasis was placed upon following rules without question, whether in doing math problems or carrying out classroom routines. Memorization of facts and copying teachers' notes off of the board dominated the social studies area. In the middle-class fifth grade, emphasis was placed upon getting the right answer in order to get a good grade. Again, facts dominated the content. Students were allowed a few choices, and some attention was given to learning how to follow directions in order to obtain the desired result. In social studies the students read assigned pages and answered teacher questions. In both types of schools passivity and conformity dominated. In these schools, subjects were lifeless accumulations of facts that were to be mastered, meaning memorized.

In contrast, content was something quite different and the students engaged it differently in the affluent professional and executive elite schools. Emphasis in the affluent professional fifth grade was on independent, creative activity. Students were given choices and continually asked to express and justify their opinions. "Work involves individual thought and expressiveness, expansion and illustration of ideas, and choice of appropriate method and material."[14] The social studies area involved young people in "illustrating and re-creating the culture of the people of ancient times."[15] It also included the study and sharing of current events. For these children content was flexible, accessible, something to be played with and explored. "In the executive elite school, work is developing one's analytical intellectual powers. Children are continually asked to reason through a problem, to produce intellectual products that are both logically sound and of top academic quality. A primary goal of thought is to conceptualize rules by which elements may fit together in systems, and then to apply these rules in solving a problem. School work helps one to achieve, to excel, to prepare for life."[16] For these affluent children, content was not so much to be played with, but to be used and manipulated to realize their personal aims. Mastery of content was a source of personal power.

The quantity of content also varies. Lower- and working-class children generally receive far fewer opportunities to interact with academic subject matter in comparison with their better off peers. Through tracking, some young people actually spend thousands of hours more being exposed to the organized experience of the human race than other young people who accumulate graduation credits through taking business mathematics, foods courses, and through work experience; some kids take calculus while others end their encounter with mathematics at something called pre-algebra. But, even within heterogeneously grouped classrooms, there are vast differences in opportunities to engage content.

Young people within the same classrooms are treated very differently. Those who teachers perceive as able are more likely to be given opportunities to engage content actively, while most children are taught the lie directly. Students who are seen as bright and able are more often praised than their less able peers for correct responses. They are more likely to have a teacher give them additional time when asked to answer a question and additional feedback on the quality of the response. They receive more eye contact and more positive nonverbal interaction, such as a smile. They are more likely to have the opportunity to engage in assignments emphasizing meaning and concepts while their less able classmates are more likely to engage in drill and practice. Students perceived as less able are likely to be asked to do less work and to receive praise for marginal or inadequate performance. They are also less likely to be called on and more likely to be criticized for incorrect public responses.[17] One result appears to be that the less able become less able; the more able become more able, and get more and better quality content. Clearly, this should not be so.

How school knowledge is divided and allocated throughout the curriculum has helped make certain that school content will be generally of poor quality, limited quantity, and lifeless. Aside from the insistence that content be neatly packaged into courses and units, perhaps the greatest insult to the inquisitive mind is the survey course. The survey course begins its assault on the minds of young people in the early grades, but it is especially pronounced in the junior and senior high school. The goal of such courses is always the same, "coverage." There is a large, mythical, and shockingly flimsy, patchwork quilt that includes all the important names and dates of American and world history, all the essential rules of Algebra, and all the major genres of English literature that is tossed over the heads of all American students, many of whom suffocate under the load. There is always too much to be covered and never enough time; superficiality reigns supreme. Time, the teacher's nemesis, dictates what will be covered as well as how. An educationally desirable activity will be passed over if it requires too much time—time taken away from some other topic that presumably "must be taught."

What content is, how young people are allowed to engage it, its quality and quantity, all differ, then, for different kinds of children. If Americans have any interest in educational quality, we need to look behind statements of credit to find out what kind of content (and what kind of interaction a young person has had with it) that is represented by three units of English or perhaps two of science. It is not the credits that are important, but rather the experience had in gaining them, and whether or not these experiences accurately reflect all that is thought necessary to becoming generally educated.

But why is this important? Why should Americans care? If, as is widely claimed, a central aim of public schooling is to prepare young people, *all young people*, for full social participation, then the only reasonable and just approach to education is to provide *all* the opportunity to gain *all* of the skills and understanding essential to participation not only within a narrow economic realm, but within the wider public arena as well. And children deserve the opportunity to experience all of the basic kinds of encounters with high quality content that have proven to be rich avenues for individual development over the course of human history. Such was the view of the Supreme Court in the landmark decision of Brown vs. Topeka Board of Education in 1954: "Where a state has undertaken to provide a benefit to the people, such as public education, the benefits must be provided on equal terms to all the people unless the state can demonstrate a compelling reason for doing otherwise." Because the economy requires garbage collectors as well as professors, is not a compelling reason for unequal treatment.

The old adage is true, knowledge is power—as students in executive elite schools come to realize as they mature. Participation requires that young people possess intellectual power in the form of a wide range of skills—analytical, linguistic, technical—and understanding, which are comparatively unimportant if the purpose of the public school is to prepare young people to fit into different slots within society. In this view, it is reasonable to prepare them differentially; some students will be given the opportunity to develop one set of skills and understandings which may lead to the corridors of power atop the social pyramid, other students will get something less.

Public schools must provide the young with the tools necessary for the wise exercise of power in its many forms. This includes opportunities to gain an insider's understanding of how our society operates, of how knowledge is created and manipulated, and of how power is established and maintained. Perceiving content as it is presented in the executive elite school—as open, flexible, and susceptible to manipulation and control—is an essential element in gaining such understanding. To do this requires that opportunities be given to apply the concepts, principles, and generalizations taught in school to the study of individual and community life. School courses, especially in the social studies area, must reach out beyond the school walls. This is an essential part of developing an intimate acquaintance with the ideals that have historically inspired Americans to action, just as it is fundamental to overcoming the gulf that separates the school from the public world. In sum, school knowledge is a kind of symbolic capital that may lead to cultural, social, and perhaps even physical capital, each being avenues of power that can be restricted or broadened. It is only reasonable, therefore, that all young people be given access to the same quality and quantity of content, and opportunities to use it in ways that will expand their power. But, because students learn differently, there will necessarily be some variation in how access is given.

Changing how content is understood, improving its quality and quantity, and broadening the ways in which young people are allowed to engage it, will require a revolution in American education. There are, happily, some hopeful signs on the horizon; some educators are taking action on these issues. One example comes from California, where Bill Honig, state superintendent of public instruction, and his colleagues are forcing textbook publishers to improve the quality of their materials. Superintendent Honig's reaction to the poor quality of textbooks caught publishers by surprise: "We've heard a number of times that things were going to change, only to see them fall apart down the road."[18] This time, however, things were different. In September 1985 the state school board "notified eight publishers that it would not accept in present form the junior high science texts they offered for adoption," not one of them. "The reason: inadequate treatment of human reproduction, ethics (in treating subjects like pollution) and, most glaringly, evolution. The state's 16-member curriculum commission charged that these topics 'were systematically omitted from the vast majority of textbooks.' " The six "least neglectful publishers" were given a month to submit "acceptable revision plans," which they did, and better materials were the result. Other states would do well to follow California's lead; young people have a right to read texts that are literate, and represent the best that we know.

THE ROLE OF HIGHER EDUCATION

Much of the blame for the poor quality of the content we find in our schools can be squarely placed upon American higher education. Our colleges and universities have consistently neglected teacher education, while simultaneously and inappropriately forcing its aims and means upon the public schools. Happily, however, even here there are a few hopeful signs. In many higher education institutions across the country, like my own, there is emerging a heightened awareness of the generally poor quality of the educational experience offered to undergraduate students where programs are poorly organized, knowledge is fragmented, and teaching dominated by the lecture. Poorly educated teachers are not alone in their disatisfaction with higher education and happily, higher education is beginning to respond.

In addition to the wide range of efforts being directed toward the improvement of the undergraduate experience, there are specific reform efforts aimed at the education of future teachers. Teacher education is commonly thought of as composed of three types of education: liberal or general, professional, and specialized or discipline centered. About a fourth of the courses taken by prospective secondary education teachers fall into the second category, and about a third into the final category. The reason for this is that students planning to teach in the secondary schools, with very few exceptions, obtain academic majors and minors. Elementary education students, in contrast, usually obtain education degrees and complete comparatively fewer academic requirements. The rest of a student's program is filled up with general or liberal education courses. In both cases, better teachers will come from better encounters with high-quality content in each of the three areas. None can be ignored with impunity.

The past few years professional schools of education have been under attack and are only now beginning to respond forthrightly. They are beginning to accept their portion of blame. Reports are now coming out on teacher education written by teacher educators that identify problem areas and make some bold recommendations for improvement. *Tomorrow's Teachers*, produced by the Holmes Group, a consortium of leading research university deans of education and potentially the most significant of these reports, presents an agenda for the improvement of teacher education to which the deans have committed their institutions. The general goals are to (1) make the education of teachers intellectually more solid; (2) recognize differences in teachers' knowledge, skill, and commitment, in their education, certification, and work; (3) create standards of entry to the profession—examinations and educational requirements—that are professionally relevant and intellectually defensible; (4) connect Holmes institutions to schools; and (5) make schools better places for teachers to work, and to learn.[19]

From these general goals several specific recommendations flow along with standards of acceptable performance. For this discussion two points are of particular significance. The first is that Holmes Group institutions are committed to cleaning up their own acts. To do this will require that, contrary to current practices, courses on teaching must become research based. Students of teacher education need to know, for instance, what has been shared in this chapter, that studies have shown that young people perceived as having lower ability are frequently treated by teachers in ways that reinforce rather than challenge their weaknesses. Becoming aware of research of this kind, along with that related to how to best organize content for presentation, and much more, is a first and necessary step toward improved practice. Teachers must become students of teaching. The second is that Holmes Group instititions agree with the general criticism that many teachers have not spent enough time studying the content areas they are to teach and therefore recommend that teacher education become a postgraduate study so that more attention can be given to the disciplines of knowledge. Realizing, however, that more time spent under current conditions is likely to lead to little if any improvement, Holmes Group members are committed to working with faculty members in the disciplines and those who teach general education courses to improve the quality of the education offered. How can we expect teachers to present a view of content as flexible, open, dynamic, and alive if they do not, themselves, possess this understanding?

The entire system of higher education is to blame for the current understanding teachers possess of the nature of knowledge. "Our own professional schools are part of the problem. . . . The many badly taught and often mindlessly required courses that our students, like all undergraduates, must take in the various departments of arts, sciences, and humanities, . . .

the weak pedagogy, the preoccupation with 'covering the material,' the proliferation of multiple-choice tests, and the delegation of much teaching to graduate students—increasingly, students who cannot speak English very well"—all indicate our misplaced emphasis in education. "We [the Holmes Group members] are pressing ahead with our own faculties, and will continue. But American colleges and universities must get to work on these larger problems of teacher education."[20] Further, "If teachers are to know a subject so that they can teach it well, they need to be taught it well; . . . most undergraduates need both good pedagogy and courses that help them to learn the structure of the subjects they will teach. Neither is common today."[21] Though the jury will not come in for perhaps another five years, the effort of the Holmes Group and others, like the Carnegie Forum, suggests a heightening of awareness of the content-related problems of the public schools and indicates, hopefully, a greater willingness than has been seen in some years to do something about the situation.[22] On their part, university students have a right to a decent education and they should not hesitate to press their claims upon recalcitrant faculty.

An additional word should be said about the composition of the majors and minors offered on university campuses. Currently, with the exception of elementary education, which, unfortunately, is a major, teachers take basically the same courses as any other students of English, language, and so forth. But, they suffer from additional problems. Reflecting faculty strengths and interests, such programs are highly specialized and terribly disjointed. The aim of university faculty is to produce people just like themselves, specialists in the disciplines who have the potential to add to the body of accumulated knowledge. Typically, they are not overly fond of students who want to be teachers. It is especially hard for them to understand why a promising student of biology, for example, would want to teach; such a person is a traitor to the disciplines. Even while ridiculing the poor quality of students who come to them from the public schools, faculty are loath to get involved in improving the education offered to future teachers. They are especially reluctant to consider reforming their program requirements to make certain that future teachers do significant work in the content areas they will actually be teaching. Currently, a beginning teacher fresh from the university with a degree in biology may be expected to teach general life sciences, perhaps wildlife and maybe botany, physiology, zoology, or advanced biology. It is very likely that this student is only minimally prepared to teach any of these areas and will have to learn the content on the job. Although common, this is inexcusable.

Teaching majors ought to be different in significant ways from nonteaching majors, and it is the responsibility of university faculty to make certain this change occurs. The university content taught should be more closely related to public school content, but, in addition, special attention should be given to help teachers develop an intimate acquaintance with the structure and modes of inquiry that characterize the disciplines. The disciplines need to be enlivened for teachers or they will never be so for young people. Such knowledge is essential to breaking the textbook stranglehold; an ignorant teacher is a dependent one.

EXPOSURE TO KNOWLEDGE AND HUMAN EXPERIENCE

Better materials and better education for teachers will go a long way toward improving school content, but these alone are insufficient means for solving the problem before us. In addition to making certain that all young people spend more time studying the organized experience of the human race, educators need to make certain they are also engaging this experience and applying it in ways most likely to connect to individual experience. Facts, concepts, generalizations, and principles, the stuff of the disciplines, are made fully meaningful when applied to the study of genuine problems. Learning a content area is, therefore, not so much a grand exercise in trivial pursuits—the accumulation of facts—but rather an occasion to enter into a world of compelling and enduring problems, issues, and concerns that form the agendas of the historian, physicist, and social scientist.

To become generally educated it is not necessary for a student to be able to think just like specialists in each of the disciplines; this aim is a source of the fragmentation of the university curriculum. It is, however, necessary for the young person to be able to appropriately engage content in broad areas that reflect the range of our species' collective experience. It is at this point, once again, that Adler's views, as presented in the *Paideia Proposal*, and expanded upon in chapter two, help us. He argues that young people need to be coached in skill development, and engage in socratic dialogue, as well as be given necessary background information. English, social studies (which includes history), mathematics, and science are the common academic threads that run across the curriculum. At each stage, all young people should be guaranteed that at least some of their courses in these areas will coach them in the modes of inquiry, help them learn how to pose questions of what is usually taken for granted. What I have in mind here is roughly analogous to what several universities are now doing with the teaching of writing. In order to graduate, all students must complete a certain number of courses designated as "writing intensive." The content of these courses includes the coaching of writing. Similarly, all young people ought to be enrolled in courses that coach them in mathematical thinking, scientific inquiry, and so on. The aim is to gain a taste of the inner workings of the disciplines not for the purpose of becoming junior physicists, but rather to gain an understanding of what physicists do, the problems that concern them, the questions they pose, and their impact on our collective being. Other courses may appropriately focus more on making certain that students have the background information deemed essential for becoming generally educated, but in these courses the aim is different, just as is the content. Depth replaces breadth of coverage. Concepts, generalizations, and principles are seen in relationship to the problems and modes of inquiry that lead to their creation.

Social studies will serve as an example. In the elementary school many teachers introduce youngsters to social studies through lessons on understanding self and others. By the middle grades community needs such as health are commonly studied.[23] The fourth grade includes more formal attention to history in the form of the study of the exploration and colonization of the United States. The themes of history, geography, and civics characterize the social studies by the fifth and sixth grades.

Overall, social studies in the elementary school is varied and idiosyncratic in contrast to the general uniformity that emerges at the junior and senior high school levels. In junior high, young people study United States history, world history, world geography, and frequently a course in state history. In the senior high, American history and government are most common along with the opportunity to take selected electives such as sociology or economics.

Teachers hold some lofty goals for these classes: young people are expected to understand relationships, draw inferences and conclusions, and understand cause and effect relationships. They are also supposed to develop a variety of skills including map reading, note taking, and the ability to use dictionaries and encyclopedias.[24] Unfortunately, judging from the tests kids take, in practice these goals are infrequently achieved. Recall what is tested: in 1492 Columbus sailed the ocean blue. Multiple choice, true-false, fill-in-the-blank, and matching test questions dominate. Moreover, the texts used portray a "kind of remoteness or detachment from real people living in a time and a place."[25] Topics are "removed from their intrinsically human character"; shrivelled and distorted, they are reduced to easily forgotten dates and places.[26] Accordingly, the public world is studied at a distance; young people rarely venture out into the community, nor are members of the community who might give insight into its workings invited into the classroom. And, making matters even worse, topics are frequently repeated from year to year. When disconnected facts are what counts, and because no one can possibly remember them all, young people must be taught them over and over again.[27] It is little wonder that although young people are very attracted to the topics of the social studies, they do not care much for the social studies subject area itself.

If teachers are to achieve their goals for the social studies, then breadth must give way to depth of treatment; fewer topics should be studied, but studied well. And, topics must be chosen well to reflect the central interests, problems, and concerns of the community. The aim of coverage must be set aside in some courses in favor of providing quality interactions with enriched and lively content, content that speaks to the student's experience of the world. Students do not need to know every important name and date of American history to draw inferences and conclusions and to understand cause and effect relationships. They must, however, study topics in ways that allow them to engage in these kinds of intellectual operations. Such outcomes cannot be achieved by superficially engaging poor quality content. Nor does learning of this kind come from the avoidance of controversy.

Intuitively, many elementary teachers have been on the mark when teaching the social studies. They have begun by having children study topics close at hand, the family for instance. Unfortunately, from this good beginning a gigantic leap is made from the personal to the impersonal. Suddenly, when studied formally, the social studies is about other people, usually dead people, and their problems. The transition that is necessary, especially if the aim is to help young people begin to see themselves as history makers and as part of the public world, comes when young people are allowed to do sociology, psychology, economics, and history, albeit, amateurishly. They begin by writing the history of an important event close to their own lives, perhaps the events surrounding their birth. They interview participants, review primary source material, and write up an interpretation. From here they move out into the world to study events that influenced their lives — ones they did not participate in directly, but know someone who did. This, too, is studied and written about: the Battle of Iwo Jima, for instance. The aim is not the accumulation of systematic historical information, but rather knowledge of the ethical principles, problems, and modes of inquiry associated with historical study.

South Carolina appears to be making headway in this direction. Very soon part of the history requirements for all eighth graders in the state will be to participate in an ongoing oral history project. Every student will have the opportunity to interview a person who has been part of South Carolina's history. There are potential dangers in a project of this kind; it may turn out to be nothing more than a glorification of local history. But, if done properly, it may be a means for young people to begin to see themselves as history makers. And, it may be an important means for helping them understand the role of social theory and interpretation in historical writing.

The principle of depth over breadth should also shape instructional decisions in American government courses. On the face of it, I have a difficult time imagining how either the Declaration of Independance or the Constitution can be made boring and irrelevant, but they can be. When taught as part of a survey course, there simply is not enough time to spend actually studying these documents and their origins; the two most important pieces of writing to Americans, knowledge of which is essential for our education, are made lifeless, treated and tested like any other bits of information. In order to pump life back into them, these documents must be studied in terms of their impact on the lives of us all. To do this, of course, requires that we have teachers who can give life and love to these documents. And this requires they be educated differently.

We have come full circle. Those charged with teacher education, in the disciplines and in schools of education, have their work cut out for them. Teachers must be given access to better content and different kinds of content, and helped to develop the skills and understandings necessary for connecting the experience of the race with the individual experience of young people. But, this is only part of the solution. In this chapter I have stressed curricular reorganization but other changes, touched on in previous chapters, are also necessary. Two are of special importance: teachers must be given a much greater say over curriculum decisions, and standardized testing, which places such a high premium on mastery of poor quality content, must be deemphasized.

7

Creativity and Schooling

THE NEVERENDING STORY[1] is an enchanting tale about Bastian Balthazar Bux, a small, fat, timid boy, and his struggle to believe in an imaginary land that is more than imaginary. His classmates delight in teasing Bastian, who lives in constant fear of them. One day, while trying to escape the school bullies, Bastian takes refuge in a cluttered bookstore operated by Mr. Coreander, a strange, crusty old man who has little fondness for children. Bastian has interrupted Mr. Coreander's reading. Irritably he tells the boy that children know nothing of books and he wonders why one of them is defiling his sanctuary. Bastian protests: he is not like other children. The old man pauses, surprised, wondering if perhaps standing before him *is* a different kind of child. They talk, the phone rings and Bastian is left alone momentarily. The shimmering copper-colored, silk-covered book that Mr. Coreander was reading strangely attracts Bastian, who thumbs through it while a passion grows; he must have that book! Heart pounding, Bastian clutches the book to his chest and quietly retreats from the bookstore before Mr. Coreander returns, making certain the bells on the door do not give him away. Once out of the store he runs wildly away. In panic he realizes he is a thief with no where to go. He cannot go home. Regaining his composure, Bastian discovers that out of habit he has gone to school.

> At every step he felt the fear rising within him. Under the best of circumstances he was afraid of school, the place of his daily defeats, afraid of his teachers, who gently ap-

pealed to his conscience or made him the butt of their
rages, afraid of the other children, who made fun of him
and never missed a chance to show him how clumsy and
defenseless he was. He had always thought of his school
years as a prison term with no end in sight, a misery that
would continue until he grew up, something he would just
have to live through.

But when he now passed through the echoing corridors with their smell of floor wax and wet overcoats, when
the lurking stillness suddenly stopped his ears like cotton,
and when at last he reached the door of his classroom,
which was painted the same old-spinach color as the walls
around it, he realized that this, too, was no place for him.
He would have to go away. So he might as well go at once.[2]

Bastian remembers the vacant school attic where he will be
safe. While his classmates grind away, Bastian, surrounded by
dusty and discarded objects of learning, begins reading about
Fantastica. Fantastica is in danger of The Nothing which slowly
consumes all before it, even the mountainous but gentle giant
rock chewers and Morla, the ancient turtle. For those who survive their initial encounter with The Nothing, as did three bark
trolls, there is no pain, "There's just something missing. And
once it gets hold of you, something more is missing every day."
Soon, "nothing" is all that is left. If The Nothing is not stopped,
the Ivory Tower will be destroyed as will the frail childlike empress at whose death all of Fantastica ceases to be. There is but
one hope for salvation: if Atreyu, a small warrior-boy, can find
a child from the Outer World, our world, who is willing, because of believing so fully in Fantastica, to go with Atreyu to the
Empress to give her a new name. Atreyu's quest is a difficult
one. Unfortunately, as Uyulala the Oracle tells Atreyu, mortal
children have not visited Fantastica in a good long while, "for
they no longer know the way. . . . They don't believe in us any
more. . . . For theirs is the world of reality."[3]

As Bastian follows Atreyu's quest, he realizes that he might
be the child being sought. " 'Yes! yes!' Bastian shouted. Then,
terrified of his own voice, he added more softly: 'I'd go and help
you if I knew how. I don't know the way, Atreyu. I honestly
don't.' "[4] Besides, how can Bastian help? He is a fat, weak, little

boy, not a grown warrior, who has skipped school to do some reading. Moreover, it is only a story. But, Bastian comes to understand that it is more than just a story. "He . . . realized that not only was Fantastica sick, but the human world as well. The two were connected. He had always felt this, though he could not have explained why it was so. He had never been willing to believe that life had to be as gray and dull as people claimed. He heard them saying: 'Life is like that,' but he couldn't agree. He never stopped believing in mysteries and miracles."[5] In this belief he continues with Atreyu, but hesitates, as his courage fails him. It is only after a desperate struggle, when the "neverending story" becomes Bastian's story, that he is able to help save Fantastica. "Close to fainting, he suddenly cried out: 'Moon Child, I'm coming!' "[6] And, with the new name, Fantastica is "born again" from Bastian's wishes.[7] Through this act of courage, Bastian discovers within himself a strong, able person, a person who can re-create the world.

Eventually, Bastian Balthazar Bux finds his way out of the story, which is nearly as difficult as getting there. To do so he must recover a "forgotten dream" that will guide him back to his world and to the most fundamental values of life.[8] He finds this dream, and suddenly is returned to the cold, damp school attic, back to reality, but it is a different reality. Bastian's world has changed; he will never again see through the eyes of a frightened little fat boy.

Back in the attic Bastian begins wondering, how long has he been in Fantastica? He reaches for the book only to discover that it is gone, nowhere to be found. At home, he is greeted by his waiting father, gravely concerned and wanting to know where his weary son has been. Bastian takes a risk: "he told the whole story in great detail. It took many hours. [But his] father listened as he had never listened before. He understood Bastian's story."[9]

The next day the boy musters up the courage to confess his crime to Mr. Coreander who surprises Bastian by telling him that nothing was taken, no book was missing. Mr. Coreander too, wants to hear Bastian's story. At the conclusion of the tale, the bookdealer, who himself has visited Fantastica, tells Bastian that "Every real story is a Neverending Story. . . . There are many doors to Fantastica, my boy. There are other such magic books. A lot of people read them without noticing. It all depends on who gets his hands on such books." Bastian asks: " 'Then the Neverending Story is different for different people?' 'That's right . . . And besides, it's not just books. There are other ways of getting to Fantastica and back. You'll find out.' "[10]

Bastian's story as a student most certainly continued. I imagine him facing his teacher, first day back to school following his adventure: he tells her that he missed class because he was visiting Fantastica and riding Falkor, the luckdragon. "Of course," the teacher says, "but you should be in school, Bastian. You've much to learn." Later that day she talks with the school psychologist over lunch about Bastian and expresses her concern that he does not seem to be able to face up to responsibility and has a terrible time telling his imaginary world apart from the real world. He lacks friends and is always getting into trouble with the other kids. "He really doesn't even know," she tells the psychologist, "when he is lying." The psychologist assures the teacher that she will meet with the boy very soon to discuss his problem. Unfortunately, it will be a few days before they can meet because she has so many other children that must be counseled first and Bastian's problem is not really disrupting the class.

Bastian's assessment that the public world and the inner world of creativity are intimately intertwined seems reasonable. The revitalization of the public world, is bound tightly to the cultivation of creativity in its many and varied forms. In the words of the Carnegie Forum,

> The skills needed now are not routine. Our economy will be increasingly dependent on people who have a good intuitive grasp of the ways in which all kinds of physical and social systems work. They must possess a feeling for mathematical concepts and the ways in which they can be applied to difficult problems, an ability to see patterns of meaning where others see only confusion; a cultivated creativity that leads them to new problems, new products and new services before their competitors get to them; and,

in many cases, the ability to work with other people in
complex organizational environments where work groups
must decide for themselves how to get the job done.[11]

It is to those with childlike curiosity and "cultivated creativity" that we look for new ways of seeing and being in the world,
those who have not lost the ability to "dip into their . . . stores
of pleasure and fantasy" and thereby reveal to the rest of us
unexpected visions of possibility and wonder.[12] To these individuals the world is not to be taken for granted; it is open, vulnerable, and wonderous. The world comes to them filled with problems awaiting definition and solution; reality rests upon a
question mark, not a period. To the rest of us, those whose
capacity to wonder and to act unexpectedly has been dulled by
living in and being consumed by external reality, it is something
quite different. It simply *is*. As such it is reflected in what we
feel, hope for, believe, and understand. It is a clear lens through
which we interpret our experience, an invisible filter through
which we define our problems and establish what solutions are
possible and reasonable.

Schooling plays an important role in either enhancing or
retarding the development of creativity. Generally, schooling is
dulling. It is in the attic where Bastian's imagination may dance
freely, not in the classroom. For the most part, schooling is
dedicated to establishing boundaries of what is proper behavior
or understanding, including the mastery of skills and traditions.
Education, however, should be something more than schooling,
it should include opportunities to go through tradition and beyond to see new possibilities in old worlds. To be educated is to
be able to locate and correct difficences in our understanding of
the world. It is to see how our actions ripple outward to influence the lives of those far removed from us in space and time.
It is to recognize and celebrate the tentativeness and incomplete-
ness of experience and understanding. It is to be open to experience that is contradictory to the taken for granted. And, it is to
have eyes open to a changing landscape of feeling, fact and
understanding.

Schooling gives creativity a rough time. Two examples come
to mind from preschool classes, where one would expect

children to be allowed to express themselves freely and openly. Last year I attended a conference with the preschool teachers of our four-year-old son. They liked Seth, saying that he was a delightful child who enjoyed making up elaborate fantasies and sharing them with the teachers and other children. After listening to them sing his praises, I asked if they thought he had any problems that his mother and I ought to know about. Silence followed. Then one teacher, apologetically, mentioned that he had difficulty distinguishing his stories from external reality, they blended into one another as in a rainbow orange slips into red. The other teacher laughed a bit uncomfortably and nodded her assent. A second example occurred at Christmastime when our eldest son was excited about the day's project, making Santa Clauses to decorate the room. Unfortunately, no ordinary child-made Santa would do; before class the teacher carefully cut out of red and white paper the parts of the *real* Santa and then instructed the children how to glue all the pieces together. She then scurried around the room making certain that every Santa looked like every other Santa and the children dutifully tried to do exactly as they were told. The project was capped by the teacher passing out cotton balls to be glued in the appropriate places. When asked why the children could not do their own drawing, or at least cutting, the teacher matter-of-factly remarked that the parents liked identical Santas, they liked the orderliness and neatness of the room.

What both events have in common is that they reflect a denial of the individual experience and personality of young people. The aim is conformity to preestablished, rigid, standards. These are not at all unusual events, however. After all, as discussed in chapter two, schools are designed to make "good students" — highly verbal, conforming, and dutiful young people. We all have had similar experiences. I have witnessed events of this kind in art classes in the elementary grades, in mathematics, in social studies, in which there has been a systematic and well-documented denial of the cultural experience of young people, and in reading. Deficiency is located in the individual's experience and personality, not in either the content (experience of the race) or in the teacher's understanding or presentation of it. To be a good student a denial of self is required; the student's aim is to establish congruity between his or her own experience and interpretation of the world, and that which is officially sanctioned—the world is taken as given with the result that it is disconnected from young people. To imagine things not as they are is to be foolish; through schooling young people are prepared for life by being required to deny life.

Situations of this kind arise not only because of individual teacher decisions and attitudes but also because of the nature of schooling itself. As noted in chapter six, public schooling fragments knowledge and experience. Reflecting values of the marketplace, courses are neatly packaged into adminstratively convenient blocks of time that have nothing to do with the nature of human learning. Moreover, the senses are constantly assaulted by swarming crowds, bells, grades, and a myriad of other reminders of an external reality hostile to the individual.

In our quest to reform American public education, one of our priorities ought to be to establish the conditions necessary for the cultivation of creativity. Happily, through studies of creativity, we are beginning to understand a great deal about what kinds of environments foster it and how creativity establishes connections between the private world of experience and the public world. Perhaps the most important recent study is *Notebooks of the Mind,* which focuses on how a large group of creative men and women, who are characterized as "experienced and productive thinkers," think.[13] That attention is paid to creative women sets this study apart from others. Through interviews, published accounts of how creative people think, and analyses of their work, the author, Vera John-Steiner, attempts to understand what is distinctive about these individuals' thought processes and how they got that way. There are important implications in this work for schooling and for the re-creation of the public world.

To frame her insights it is first necessary to briefly address her concluding question: is creativity a matter of nature or nurture? Perhaps most Americans assume that creativity is a matter of being born to it, it is in the genes. Certainly, to some unknown degree this is true. But, too often the view is that genes are destiny. Far too little attention has been paid to environmental factors. As John-Steiner reminds us, "creative work is rooted in the material conditions of existence, such as space, money, and experience."[14] It makes a great deal of difference if a child is born to a wealthy, intellectually active and supportive set of parents or a poor, illiterate, single mother. True, occasionally talent does surface under even the most dire circumstances, but for each story of this kind there are unimaginable numbers of untold stories of failure.

Ultimately, it probably matters little whether nature or nurture is of most signficance. What is important is that schools can and do make a difference. Unfortunately, however, this difference frequently comes about only because of a single, remarkable teacher, rather than as a result of an institutionwide commitment. James Baldwin, for example, had such a remarkable teacher, a woman the students called "Bill Miller":

> She had directed my first play and endured my first theatrical tantrums and had then decided to escort me into the world.[15]

The burden is to establish throughout American schools the conditions and commitment necessary for the emergence and cultivation of creativity so that all children may become increasingly what they are fundamentally by nature—inquisitive, wondering, problem solvers who seek connections with others and the world through a wide variety of expressive mediums.

Before describing some of these conditions, it will be helpful to briefly describe the qualities of mind that we hope to cultivate. The first is continuity, which John-Steiner characterizes as sustained commitment, as continuity between inner and outer life. "The full realization of generative ideas requires a sustained, often painful, dialectic between condensed inner thoughts and realization."[16] Creative persons tend to be preoccupied with the ideas or projects at hand. For them there is little distinction between work and play. Intensity expressed as passion for one's task and courage—a willingness to take risks, to play out hunches and go public with the results—are two related and important additional qualities. As noted in chapter two, these qualities are too seldom found even among our better students. Yet another quality is openness to experience: "Creative individuals' openness to all their feelings and reactions distinguish them . . . from others less able to confront their emotions."[17] When linked with courage, openness makes it possible to learn from mistakes, which become challenges to be overcome rather than moments of profound embarrassment to be avoided at all costs.

Two additional qualities are imagination and curiosity. Imagination, the ability to see things not as they are, is the source of fantasy and humor, as well as fresh categories for reorganizing experience. Sometimes, imagination expresses itself as a flight from the mundane, a muffled protest against external reality. Einstein said that "one of the strongest motives that lead persons to art and science is flight from every day life, with its painful harshness and wretched dreariness, and from the fetters of one's shifting desires."[18] Curiosity is the desire to get under surface appearances. "The search for going beneath the appearance of things . . . is shared by those who unconsciously get purposefully prepared for a life of the mind whether in the sciences or the arts. But at the beginning, all that the young . . . [seem] to be aware of is a great love of the uncommon."[19] Curiosity expresses itself as a playful attitude toward ideas, an attitude associated with instruction of upper-class children (as noted in the preceeding chapter) and present in virtually all small children. Ideas are like toys to be broken apart and reassembled, to be used as not intended, to be combined with other toys to make even grander creations, and then to be disregarded and abandoned when the magic they once had departs.

In cultivating continuity, intensity or passion, courage, openness, curiosity, and imagination, a fine line must be straddled as Getzels and Jackson suggest.[20] In the spirit of general education, a tolerable balance is the goal otherwise creativity may actually be crushed. Imagination can turn into flights of fantasy and withdrawl from the public world. Passion can become rigidity. Openness may become rootlessness and naive relativity. Courage can move past independence of mind and into unruliness and rebellion. As we consider the conditions most likely to foster creativity these dangers must be kept in mind.

John-Steiner identifies a number of environmental elements that are likely to cultivate creativity. Speaking developmentally, the task is to create the conditions most likely to turn the wondering child into the passionate, yet disciplined, innovative problem-solver. In this process, mentors and apprenticeships are especially important, as James Baldwin testified. While oftentimes the mentor is a parent, friend or relative, sometimes it is a teacher. In any case, there is no substitute for an interested and able adult with whom the novice can apprentice to be nurtured and to learn the inner logic and craft of the particular form of expressiveness being explored whether science, dance, writing, or music. Support is of great importance because the individual can never quite achieve what is imagined, so discouragement frequently follows. "The contradictory pulls of joy and discouragement, of sudden bursts of insight and tiring efforts of execution, of process and product, are the necessary tensions that fuel creative thought."[21] From a mentor the student receives a "sense of direction and hope."[22] And for the more mature students, mentors offer participation in a community of shared interests. John-Steiner notes that there are other mentors in addition to the living that may be tapped, "distant teachers" as she calls them, such as Shakespeare or Milton, whose works serve as models for study and emulation.[23] In effect, these are intellectual and artistic heroes who beckon us to new heights of understanding and expressiveness.

Exposure to and immersion in the various forms of human expressiveness are also necessary elements in the development of creativity. Obviously, if a young person does not know physics exists, he or she cannot aspire to become a physicist. The issue here is not just one of providing opportunity, however, it is also a question of the quality of the exposure as noted in the preceeding chapter. Schools need to be closely linked with representatives of the various communities of expressiveness. Involvement in the public schools of artists, scientists, and others noted for their imaginative accomplishments should become more commonplace.

Freedom is another element. Obviously, young people cannot simply be turned loose, as Getzels and Jackson remind us, to do whatever they will. As argued in preceeding chapters, the education of young people should be carefully structured. But, within this structure, room must be made for young people to explore their own questions individually and communally—

questions that arise from their experience and the study of the experience of the human race. In a spirit of trust and under careful guidance, young people must be empowered to design a portion of their own education.

The support of a mentor, exposure and immersion into the various forms of human expressiveness, and the freedom to explore experience are all tremendously important elements that ought to characterize American education but they will fall short unless connected with solid instruction. Creativity does not arise out of nothing, and it requires a prepared mind, a cultivated mind, to fully blossom. The would be mature thinker must be grounded in (but not buried by) the accomplishments of the past. In the words of Henri Cartier-Bresson,

> The potential of every human being of becoming an artist remains unfulfilled without the individual's acquaintanceship and immersion into the artistic traditions of the past, and the distinctiveness of his culture.[24]

Knowledge of methods, the modes of inquiry, the tools for making meaning developed by experienced thinkers, also is part of being grounded.

In our quest to reform American public education, one of our priorities ought to be to establish the conditions necessary for the cultivation of creativity. Although a good many of the changes needed in schooling to bring about a fuller realization of the creative capacities of young people are structural in nature (e.g., different allocations of time and other resources), individual teachers, like Bill Miller, can and do make a difference.

Teachers of the arts are most frequently looked to when the topic is the development of creativity. It is not surprising that art classes are often gathering places for "unusual" students. Certainly, the arts are particularly well suited to helping young people test the boundaries of the taken for granted or of external reality. Indeed, that they are seen as somewhat tangential to serious content is a virtue; standardized tests have not been widely adopted (although some have been developed and are in use in a few districts nationwide) and the arts are generally the only content areas within which teachers are not bound to textbooks.[25] Moreover, teachers enjoy considerable control over the arts curriculum, and, as a result, they and their students may take risks comparatively free of the fear of censorship. Not only do the arts provide means for the expression of imagination — projections of different inner and outer worlds — but such expressions are demanded by the very nature of artistic production itself. True, art problems can be posed for young people that are constraining rather than liberating — gluing red and white pieces of paper together to form Santa Clauses, or coloring a clown at the bottom of a worksheet — and technical rules may be overemphasized resulting in artistic cliches, but there is something inherently liberating in the doing of art. Creativity almost always finds a place, even if only a small one.

The responsibility for cultivating creativity, and its constituent qualities of mind and spirit, is not only that of teachers of the arts, however. It is also the responsibility of all teachers as well as others who are participating members of the various communities of experienced thinkers: scientists, historians, graphic artists, and the like. For the latter, the continued vitality of their communities depends upon a constant stream of young seekers. It is in their vital interest to make certain the stream is a vigorous one.

Opportunities to develop creativity can and should cut across the curriculum. Let us briefly consider English, for example. Most often English courses share the problems encountered within other content areas. They are disconnected from student life, particularly the internal life, for both elementary and secondary aged students. For elementary school students English is reading a primer or an anthology, doing worksheets, and perhaps book reports. For secondary school students it is doing grammar assignments and engaging in literary analysis, seeking right answers: what was Steinbeck trying to tell us in the *Grapes of Wrath*? But it can be something quite different: an encounter with distant teachers, and through writing an encounter with one's own subjectivity. The possibilities are endless. One very promising avenue for teachers in this regard is the use of young people's own stories as content.[26] Occasionally we need reminding that children's fantasies are more than silly tales; they are expressions of their attempts to understand who and what they are in relation to the world they inhabit, and to make that world their own even as they strive to transcend it.[27] The study of English provides the opportunity to read, write, and perform plays through which young people may project and test different futures, and different selves within those futures. The study of literature has long been recognized as a rich means for helping young people confront life styles and value systems fundamentally different from their own — different ways of being and knowing. Such conflicts stretch the imagination and fertilize creativity by encouraging comparisions of experience while legitimizing alternative visions of possibilility. In these and innumerable other ways young people may build a store of experiences out of which, as they become more mature thinkers, they eventually can build new worlds of understanding.

Ultimately, creativity will only flourish because it is valued and supported within the community. Within schools the signs of valuing are comparatively easy to detect. Are mentor relationships not only possible, but are those that exist acknowledged and honored? Do students encounter exemplars of the workings of imagination in person and in product? Is time available for extensive explorations of the various forms of human expressiveness, and do students have the freedom to use this time? Is there an emphasis within the curriculum and in instruction upon the problematic, the unknown, the wonderous? And are the products of creativity acclaimed publically? Even though the answer to these questions for our young, fat friend, Bastian was "no," this need not be so for us.

What I have said about developing creativity and imagination is not new to many teachers. They know and understand my words, and they know and understand the great benefits a commitment to the cultivation of creativity would have for them personally and professionally. Unfortunately, however, though they understand these things, they seldom achieve them. Part of the problem is, once again, a school structure that inhibits teachers' abilities to do what they know is best: Too many students and contrary institutional priorities make establishing the conditions for fostering creativity very difficult. But oddly, part of the problem is also due to a failure of imagination, an unwillingness or inability of educators to project a different future and a different self within that future. This is even true with the arts which too frequently are taught like any other subject area — "following the rules, finding the one right answer, practicing the lower cognitive processes."[29] Their uniqueness is forgotten even when conditions would allow them a special place within the school program. It is only as new possibilities are projected, possibilities that grow out of our experience of the world, that change capable of enhancing human values becomes realizable. Those of us concerned about education must break away from the weight of external reality, we must wake up, recapture our own pasts, and rethink what it is we ought to be doing to and for young people. The alternative is to accept a school reality that most assuredly is hostile to expressions of creativity, preferring predictability and certainty to surprise, a reality that lumbers on because of habitual institutional role playing, and forgotten experiences that now are only recalled from a dulled memory by extraordinary effort.

8

Schooling Metaphors

I N this chapter we confront perhaps the most difficult educational problem of all, a problem indirectly addressed in each chapter — the need to see American public education differently, to begin thinking in ways other than the taken for granted. In the introduction I noted that the factory has been the guiding metaphor behind American public schooling throughout this century. Through the body of the text I have dealt with a number of problems that flow from the creation and maintenance of a factory model, and I have offered suggestions about how American public education can be substantially improved. Now it is time to think about how we think about education. One way to do this is to analyze the common metaphors used in discussions of public education.

Education metaphors reveal not only how we think about issues — what is identified as a problem and what solutions are seen as reasonable — but also how we act; they channel action.[1] If the metaphors used poison imagination, as the factory metaphor and its child, the marketplace, do, then we are in desperate need of fresh metaphors by which to enrich and enliven our discourse, and to open up "fresh possibilities of thought and action."[2] We must become better able and more willing to imagine the world differently. This is revealed by eight education metaphors discussed below.

The factory metaphor contains visions of quality control and assembly line mass production. Principals are managers charged with making certain the system runs smoothly, that nothing disrupts the flow of the day. As noted, efficiency is the watchword. Teachers, as assembly line workers, are responsible for meeting, but not setting, production goals. Students are products to be molded and shaped in predetermined ways; deviation from the norm is to be avoided. Education is, therefore, something done to students.

As updated in the form of the marketplace, this metaphor and the assumptions about teaching and learning embedded in it, has dominated much of the recent reform talk just as it dominated in its earlier version reform efforts at the turn of the century. Only from this perspective can a goodly number of the current reform proposals be seen as reasonable. Among them are calls for better, more reliable and valid, testing instruments to certify product quality; for merit pay and bonuses; for increases in *individual* teacher productivity; for tighter supervision and greater conformity of teachers and students to detailed lists of behaviors that are presumably connected to increased productivity; and for greater uniformity, standardization, and rationalization of the entire school system.

Lack of efficiency in a production sense—more units for less money—is the most serious educational problem allowed by the factory metaphor. When efficiency is lacking, blame is most frequently placed on principals and teachers who are either ignorant, lazy, or unconcerned with students, and solutions usually center on altering either principal or teacher behavior; fault is rarely found in the system through which work is organized. Blame is also placed on parents for providing lousy raw material and on students for being lousy material. "What can you do," teachers commonly say, "when kids have such rotten home lives?" The answer is assumed, and obvious: nothing.

The school cannot be blamed for doing nothing with rotten material; besides quality control means that some material must be discarded because of defects. But, this does not mean that the school is necessarily callous or hard-hearted. There is room within the factory metaphor for attention to be given to a range of differences among materials. The key, however, is that these differences must fit relatively neatly into preestablished categories for treatment, parallel conveyor belts that slowly move the product toward graduation. Raw material that does not quite fit, or fits uneasily, rolls off somewhere along the line.

The most serious problem allowed by the marketplace is failure to sell a product, or, put differently, failure to supply a product the public will buy. Success results from research in the marketplace to find out precisely what services are desired and then supplying those services at a competitive price. In this process common interests are likely to be dissolved in service to special interests.

A second metaphor, especially prominent among elementary school teachers, is the school as family. In this view, the major educational problems have to do with establishing a warm, nurturing relationship with children, all children, and protecting them from the harsh realities of life. Accordingly, academic performance is less important for students than feeling good about themselves and positive toward the teacher-parent. Teachers are possessive of "their children" and resentful of job requirements that might hurt them. The necessity of grading is especially painful, and effort is weighed more heavily than actual performance.

The parent metaphor has much to commend it because the elementary school represents a transition period for young children from the family into a larger, presumably more hostile, world. As a general metaphor for thinking about schooling, however, it leaves much to be desired. There is a point at which protection and nurturance must give way to opportunities for young people to struggle with themselves and their environment in ways that will lead to a measure of power over each. Ultimately young people cannot and should not be protected from the world; rather, they must engage it.

A third metaphor embedded in how young people and junior high school teachers talk about schooling, is school as a social event and necessary evil. When interviewed about why they go to school young people overwhelmingly give social reasons, to be with their friends. They also admit that they have few other choices, they have to be in school so they might as well make the best they can of it. Junior high school teachers talk in similar ways. Young people have so many difficulties during the early teen years that the most important aspects of schooling have to do with helping them get through these years with as few scars as possible. The central educational problem is, therefore, to make schooling safe and fun.

One implication of this metaphor is that academics are reduced in importance when compared to the social life of the school. A junior high school teacher commented that "subject matter is really low on the totem pole in junior high", and she thought it should be that way. In some respects this metaphor is an extension of teacher as parent, an extension prompted by the realization that if there is no way to protect young people, there are ways of softening the blows of physical and social maturation.

School is more than a social event, just as teaching is more than being a custodian of children. Nevertheless, educationally, the social aspects of schooling are of fundamental importance and are too frequently obscured by other metaphors, most notably school as factory. One central aspect to educational reform is to pay greater, not less, attention to the kinds of relationships encouraged by schooling: are students encouraged to work together toward mutually desired aims? Are teachers rewarded for meeting together to talk about educational issues that affect the quality of school life? Are teachers rewarded for sharing ideas and materials, or discouraged from doing so? Too little attention is given to creating the conditions necessary for collegial learning relationships to be established among students and teachers.

A fourth metaphor that frequents the talk of teachers and teacher educators is the school as war zone. Talk of this kind contains a macho element. The central problems resulting from this view are for teachers, especially, but also for students, to wage the good battle, and to survive. Surviving as a teacher creates a measure of pride. The image of Sylvester Stallone storming through the hallways, encountering and quickly vanquishing student foes is appealing. A variation of this metaphor is school as zoo. Teachers are zookeepers while students are animals, funny, filthy, openly sexual, and sometimes dangerous.

The central educational problem for the zookeeper is to maintain control and a sense of humor.

School as war zone and zoo are metaphors dear to the hearts of some veteran teachers and principals who are tenuously holding on, hoping for an early retirement incentive. Education to them is a second or third order priority. Keeping the animals docile, sometimes entertained, is most important. Holding to this view makes educational reform impossible. The metaphor reflects a deep and abiding cynicism, a worship of death rather than life. Students are feared and even hated; teacher self-respect is fragile and grounded in the ability to endure the unendurable.

A fifth metaphor, one common to those who call for school reform in order to maintain our position in the international economic order, is school as marathon. Central to this belief is that education should provide an extraordinarily difficult academic course through which all young people must run. At the end of the course, a few — the strong, the brave, the worthy — will emerge triumphant. These elite few are those who will carry our banner into the economic wars of the future. Those who fall by the wayside will know they too have a part to play, but their's is a lesser calling, to support the technical-managerial elite for the good of all. From this viewpoint the task of the teacher is to identify and develop a comparatively narrow range of talent.

This marathon metaphor, one that supports programs for the gifted few, flies in the face of American democratic public education, an education dedicated to the optimal development of all and to the expansion of social participation and of power. Its appeal, however, is strong, oddly enough, even for the dispossessed. It speaks to the American fear of being second best in a nasty world, to the hope of parents that their children might assume a position in high places, and to a belief that those who get ahead deserve to do so.

A sixth metaphor, school as log, is dear to the hearts of academically housed, privately educated would be school reformers.[3] On one end of a log situated in a clearing, sits a wise and otherworldly teacher; on the opposite end sits an eager, bright, compliant student. The educational problem is simply to rid the forest of students unable or unwilling to sit still on the log. Next, it is necessary to place at the teacher's end of the log an individual selected from among the best and brightest students our colleges and universities have to offer. Lastly, it is essential that both log sitters be provided with time and resources sufficient to engage in an extended dialogue about eternal verities.

Probably everyone would like to have a turn on the log; I certainly would. But I would also like a curriculum that connects directly and forcefully to the public world, one linked to the present and future, as well as to the past. And I would like my log to be in a clearing as part of a circle of logs with a number of eager students perched upon them, which is fortunate because mass education, in any case, makes tutorials unlikley. Of all the metaphors, this one is the least connected to public education and the public world. Indeed, it reflects an attempt to escape from the world.

A seventh metaphor, drawing on futurist visions and reflecting America's fascination with technology, is school as information network. The image is one of large numbers of isolated students electronically linked to a central information bank from which they can draw upon the accumulated wisdom of our race. The problems that flow from this vision are frequently seen as only fiscal and technical: how to obtain enough terminals and computers for all students, or how to develop high quality interactive programs and the like. Rarely are questions raised of a more substantial nature. For example, what kinds of human relations are likely to result from such a heavy reliance on machines, and children learning from interaction with machines? Perhaps the most basic question is what kind of humanity will we have if this vision comes to fruition, especially given that current social relations are taken for granted by it? The technology is inherently conservative: simulations are substituted for reality; individual interaction with machines is emphasized over social discourse; and information is substituted for knowledge.

Each of the metaphors has elements that are compelling. Even the factory ideal has some virtue. It reflects a firm commitment to public education. Each, with the exception of school as factory because it is taken for granted, can extend and expand the way we think about education, teaching and learning. Yet, despite their virtues, the metaphors that inform our thinking and shape our educational visions are more constraining than liberating; unfortunately, they either give no place to the public world or offer a vision of it that is either overly romantic or cynical. In either case, the responsibility of the public school and its place within the public world is twisted and misshapen. At present we lack even a language with which to express our shared aspirations, let alone to extend them; the language of competitive individualism limits the way we think.[4] Fresher, richer, metaphors are needed, ones that reach out and link the public and private spheres.

COMMUNITY AND ITS LINK
WITH THE PUBLIC WORLD

One metaphor, more promising than the rest, in part because it arises from our collective traditions and because it connects directly with the public world and ties it to individual experience, is school as community. This is an old idea to some intellectuals, but perhaps now its time is coming. Many Americans are discovering that doing one's own thing is not enough. The quest for "purely private fulfillment is illusory: it often ends in emptiness instead."[5] This emptiness is expressed in the longing many Americans feel for the presumed commitment and connectedness of the small town.[6] It is expressed in the growing interest in things traditional, including the family. Americans are wondering, "Where is the joy?" Clearly, there is more to life than consumption.

A community is a group that has certain characteristics: first, "membership is valued as an end in itself, not merely as a means to other ends"; second, it "concerns itself with many and significant aspects of the lives of members"; third, it "allows competing factions"; fourth, its "members share commitment to common purpose and to procedures for handling conflict within the group"; fifth, its "members share responsibility for the actions of the group"; and sixth, its "members have enduring and extensive personal contact with each other."[7]

Using these criteria to judge our interactions with the world may produce some surprising results. Membership in the Democratic, Republican or Socialist parties may not mean involvement in a community. Nor does living on west 85th Street necessarily bring with it community membership, although we often think of community as synonymous with place. Neither does belonging to a union, guild, or professional association. If we pause for a moment and consider all of the groups we are involved with in some fashion, many of us will discover we are not members of any communities at all, or perhaps only members of a weak one, or only on the outskirts of a community or two. What is thought of as community turns out to be little more than a group organized to press a narrow interest, or a cluster of individuals who happen to share similar pleasures. But why should anyone care? What difference does community participation make educationally?

Society exists for three primary reasons: for the protection of citizens, for their sustenance and perpetuation, and for the development of their capacities; that is, for the purpose of education. These purposes are relevant to every stage of life; old people and young people alike need to be nourished and protected just as they require opportunities to grow and develop intellectually, ethically, and esthetically. These are not privileges to be granted to the few, but rights that come by virtue of being born human. However, with these rights come responsibilities that temper and give perspective to our cultural emphasis on the individual. These cannot be abridged without severe consequences.

Responsibility arises out of three sets of principles basic to cooperative living: empathy, justice, and reciprocity. Empathy brings with it the realization that life is capricious; there but for the grace of God go I. Justice, properly construed, demands that the least favored in our society be given the greatest assistance; we are our brother's and sister's keeper. And, reciprocity suggests that with getting, comes the responsibility to give. We all have an obligation to contribute to our collective well-being.

Society can and does make institutional provisions for the

protection, sustenance and education of its citizens. And yet, it is only through community, particular kinds of communities, that these aims can be achieved. Education is the best example. Schools are provided for the young. But schooling is not synonymous with education, although often they are confused. Becoming educated is a cradle to grave process of which formal schooling is but a part. The rest is taken care of well or poorly depending upon the kind and quality of interactions and relationships a person has, which, in turn, depend on the kind and quality of community participation. Ideally, the individual participates in a community that is dedicated to the emancipation of human capacities.

Through community, and only through community, do we become fully human: more than a selfish, egocentric, collection of appetites. We are, we exist, because we have relationships with others; our existence is fulfilled in the existence of others. It is through community that the public and private worlds are best brought together. Through community individual interests may be linked to broader human concerns that, through conflict and resolution, in turn shape and enrich our personal understanding. It is through community, building on the private world of the family, that a lively sense of the importance of empathy, justice, and reciprocity can be gained. Community is the context within which we can witness these values in operation, and develop, practice, and extend them. It is through community that our capacities are either allowed expression and enhanced, or suppressed and distorted. And, it is through community that we can engage in the kind of interaction that will result in a shared vision of the future, a vision of commitment.

For a number of years some educators and sociologists have expressed concern about the health of American communities: we are a disconnected people. In the face of rapidly expanding technology, specialization and degradation of labor, depoliticization and depersonalization of citizenship, distortion and definition of values by mass media, and all the rest of the signs of a crumbling public world that surround us, many Americans have sensed an emptiness; we are experiencing "the missing community."[8] Simultaneously, there appear to be numerous signs that we are responding to the loss by creating, voluntarily, almost spontaneously, organic groups that reflect the desire to make connections on issues that affect the quality of our lives.

Because public schooling is never neutral — it either enhances or impedes the development of the individual and of community — careful consideration needs to be given to the role of the public school in the creation and expansion of community, and the type of collective being it encourages. To do this requires exploring the criteria for community in relationship to public schooling that will, simultaneously, enable a fleshing out of the metaphor. But first, a reminder that the public school's special responsibility is to serve public purposes; therefore, the interests they reflect must be public interests, not special interests. It is the commitment to public interests that sets the school community off from many other types of communities, while linking it to some others such as nuclear disarmament groups, Common Cause, and the bruised but still vital civil rights movement.

Attendance at an American public school is not likely to bring with it community membership, although it could. Typically schools fail to meet community criteria for a number of reasons, some of them touched upon in the preceding chapters: membership is forced; little concern is shown to life outside of the classroom; competing factions are crushed rather than encouraged to openly work through differences; purposes are contradictory and confusing; competition is more valued than cooperation and collegiality; and, young people are sorted into tracks, and given different educational opportunities. In short, a gulf separates the public school from a community ideal, and from the public world, with the result that individual capacity is severely constrained. It need not be this way.

If we think of school as community, a particular kind of community, one dedicated to the emancipation of human capacities and to the enhancement of common interests, rather than as factory, marketplace, family, or any of the other metaphors, new educational possibilities open up, giving coherence to the suggestions for reform presented in preceding chapters. Let us return to the criteria for community. It is a group in which membership is valued as an end in itself and that concerns itself with the significant aspects of the lives of its members. As noted in chapter two, formal education is far from being its own end. Students attend school because they must and because, with their parents, they realize the cash value of a diploma. It would be grand if we could say that students go to school because they desperately want to be there, that they see the school as essential to their becoming fully human. Although true for some, for the vast majority of young people, school is, as noted above, a necessary evil. The aim is to accumulate all the required credits for graduation. If young people become educated along the way, all the better.

There are many reasons for this situation. I have enumerated several, including the emphasis on testing facts, on teaching passivity, on labeling and tracking, all of which encourage disengagement. But, above all of these stands the culturewide commitment to an economistic view of schooling—the factory (currently including the marketplace and all that goes with it) and a disheartening lack of interest in education other than as something taken care of by schools. Schools are simply disconnected from much of the life experience of young people, just as they are disconnected from the public and even the private worlds.

As argued in previous chapters, the challenge is to connect the school in signficant ways to the experience of the individual and to the public world—making these links is at the heart of school as community. Emphatically, the school must connect with life. There are many ways in which this can be done. Imagine school buildings containing branches of the public library, the offices of local social agencies, and preschools, for instance. Imagine students actively engaged in the on going study of questions and issues that affect the quality of their lives. Such issues as the availability of employment opportunities, the quality of child care, the effects of setting up a nuclear dump site, and a myriad of others come to mind. Imagine business and political leaders teaching classes on economics and politics. Imagine senior citizens and more mature learners working with the less mature in a wide variety of ways that tap their skills. For students the aim is a simple one. They must come to feel that participation within the school pays off in significant ways: intellectually, socially, emotionally, ethically, and aesthetically. For the rest of us the appeal of school as community is to the personal interests residing in common interests.

A community is a group that allows competing factions whose members share commitment to common purpose and to procedures for handling conflict within the group. Within a school there certainly are a variety of competing interest groups. Unfortunately, the way they are dealt with is by keeping them separate through tracking and other means. Similarly, there are significant differences among the educational views of parents. Once again, the rule is to divide and conquer. A few parents do attend back to school night, where they may privately express their concerns to teachers, but rarely do parents or students organize. An exception occurs when parents of certain types of kids, such as the severely handicapped, are brought together, often by professionals who see their own interests closely linked with providing special services. The result is a very narrow special interest group that presses its interests with little regard for anyone else's, to the detriment of unorganized parents (usually parents of children in the regular school program, which represents about 90 percent of all students, or minority children).

What is so often lacking is a vehicle for teachers and parents to engage in dialogue about the aims of education and means for getting involved. Institutionally, there is a good reason for keeping differing opinions apart: conflict is certain and disrupts the smooth flow of the day. Consider, for example, the most fundamental tension that divides us, whether we are a society dedicated to equality or meritocracy. This is an especially volatile issue that has been hidden away within the schools where it is dealt with only when it must be and then only willy-nilly. But, most of all, it is hidden from view, seldom allowed to raise its disfigured head. One means for hiding differences commonly used by beleagured educators is philosophical and psychological eclecticism. I recall, for example, attending a meeting in which the psychological basis for a new program was presented. A large chart was prominently displayed for all to see, composed of arrows leading from various "schools of psychology" toward the program. Behaviorism, gestalt, and cognitive psychology were graphically portrayed as providing the foundation for the program without any indication that these orientations are not consistent with one another. Educational jargon also helps avoid conflict by mystifying and obfuscating areas in which genuine differences may exist. If, somehow, an issue does get raised, perhaps by an angry parent, there is yet another means for avoiding conflict: experts, such as lawyers, are brought in to resolve differences with the result that no one gains in understanding but the experts.

In contrast, when community is the ideal, conflict and tension are seen as not only unavoidable but as necessary elements in becoming educated. Only through informed, open, critical, public dialogue about the aims and means of education is it possible to create agreement around a normative framework based upon the principles of empathy, justice, and reciprocity, that would allow educators, students, and parents to build a consistent and sensible educational program. The level of agreement necessary for action to take place cannot be achieved in any other way. At the school level (assuming smaller school size), teachers, parents, and students ought to engage in dialogue about the kind of educational community they wish to have within and without the school even though, for a time, the school may have to function as an island unto itself — a place in which the principles of empathy, justice, and reciprocity may find expression. A formal document ought to be written, widely disseminated, and discussed. Essential to this discussion is deciding what teachers and students can and cannot reasonably be expected to do: what ought to be the teacher, student, administrator, and parent roles within the school? Parents must be involved. Educational tasks that cannot be reasonably housed in the schools must be shifted to other agencies; education is the responsibility of everyone, not just teachers. Businesses, churches, indeed, all instititutions, should be held accountable to an educational standard.

A community is a group whose members share responsibility for the actions of the group and whose members have enduring and extensive personal contact with one another. Tracking, labeling, and age grading (separating young people into elementary, junior, and senior high schools), keep young people apart. When young people are separated, so are their parents. A common school experience, as presented earlier, along with the merging or dissolution of schooling levels, would take us a long way toward building commmunity.

Commitment from parents is more likely to come when their children will be participating in a given school for an extended period of time, six or more years, for instance. In this respect, doing away with junior high schools may make a great deal of sense. In any case, shared interests come, in part, from shared experiences; the school has an obligation to provide some of these experiences through course content, public and school service, and the critical study of common problems. In addition, shared responsibility emerges, in part, from building the opportunities to be responsible that are now sorely lacking in the schools.

The school can be an essential element in building community. By building community—through schools becoming communities—public education can best fulfill its obligations to the public world and to the individual. It is within community that the eternal contradictions between self and other, subject and object, consciousness and reality, can be resolved. And, it is within community that clashing interests can be explored and mutual understanding can be built. This said, I am not foolish enough to believe that the public schools can revitalize the public world alone, but they do have a significant part to play. The changes urged in this volume will take us part of the way. But, for even these changes to be made, many of which are quite modest, tired visions of public schooling and of education need to give way. We need to begin thinking of public education and of our responsibility to educate the young in fresh ways. Ultimately, the structure of schooling must be fundamentally changed, just as the educational responsibilities of all social institutions need to be openly acknowledged. Awareness of the weaknesses of the public school system and of distortion and confusion in our own thinking is only a first step; action must be taken. For teachers, what is at stake is a better, more educative, and reasonable professional life. For students, the promise is that passivity and docility will give way to increased personal power through active interaction with the experience of the race and with the public world. And, for Americans, in general, the hope is for a richer, more interesting and lively collective being through commitment to and greater involvement in the educative process.

NOTES

CHAPTER 1

1. Roy J. Honeywell, *The Educational Works of Thomas Jefferson* (New York: Russell and Russell, 1964), pp. 199–205.

2. *Deseret News* (Salt Lake City, Utah), 27 Jan. 1986, sec. A, p. 3.

3. Edward Krug, *The Shaping of the American High School* (New York: Harper and Row, 1964), p. 186.

4. Ibid.

5. "Help or Hoax? Vouchers Ignite a Controversy," *Time,* 2 Dec. 1985, p. 82.

6. *Deseret News* (Salt Lake City, Utah), 21 Nov. 1985, sec. A, p. 8.

7. Myron Lieberman, "Why School Reform Isn't Working," *Fortune,* 17 Feb. 1986, p. 136.

8. *New York Times,* 25 Feb. 1986, sec. D, p. 29.

9. Honeywell, *Educational Works,* p. 13.

10. Merle Curti, Willard Thorpe, and Carlos Baker, eds. (letter written to John Adams, 28 Oct. 1813), *American Issues: The Social Record* (Philadelphia: J. B. Lippincot, 1960), pp. 194–97.

11. Jonathan Mersserli, *Horace Mann: A Biography* (New York: Alfred A. Knopf, 1972).

12. See National Governor's Assoc., Center for Policy Research and Analysis, *Time for Results: The Governors' 1991 Report on Education* (August 1986).

13. Robert N. Bellah et al., *Habits of the Heart: Individualism and Commitment in American Life* (Berkeley: Univ. of California Press, 1985), p. 81.

14. Henry M. Levin and Russell W. Rumberger, *The Educational Implications of High Technology* (Stanford: Institute for Research on Educational Finance and Governance, 1983), pp. 9–10.

15. *New York Times,* 6 Sept. 1985, sec. A, p. 15.

16. *New York Times,* 21 Sept. 1985, sec. A, p. 1.

17. Bellah, *Habits of the Heart,* p. 191.

18. Ibid., p. 271.

19. Ibid., p. 82.

20. Ibid., p. 271.

21. A recent study of the distribution of wealth among American families, commissioned by the Federal Reserve Board and conducted at the University of Michigan, concludes that the "wealthiest top 10 percent of the families in the United States — 7.5 million households — own 84 percent of the nation's assets." Even worse, "the richest one percent — 840,000 households — own half of the country's wealth, currently estimated at $10.6 trillion." *Deseret News,* Salt Lake City, Utah), 27 Sept. 1986, sec. A, p. 6.

22. Bellah, *Habits of the Heart,* p. 60.

23. A similar point is made by Michael Krashinsky: "Vouchers have not been adopted because voters are concerned about protecting the public interest in education when it is produced in a competitive market." *See* "Why Education Vouchers May Be Bad Economics," *Teachers College Record* 88 (Winter 1986): p. 149.

24. See Harry Braverman, *Labor and Monopoly Capital* (New York: Monthly Review Press, 1974).

25. Bellah, *Habits of the Heart,* p. 148.

26. Ibid., p. 267.

27. Bellah discusses these and other local efforts, including religious ones, to cultivate civic virtue. See Ibid., p. 214.

28. Elizabeth Greene, *Chronicle of Higher Education* vol. 33, no. 19 (21 Jan. 1987), p. 1.

29. R. Freeman Butts, *The Revival of Civic Learning: A Rationale for Citizenship Education in American Schools,* (Phi Delta Kappa Educational Foundation, 1980), p. 114.

CHAPTER 2

1. "Excerpts from Newman's Report on Higher-Education Policy," *The Chronicle of Higher Education* vol. 21, no. 3 (18 Sept. 1985): p. 22.

2. Ibid., p. 21.

3. Ibid.

4. John I. Goodlad, *A Place Called School: Prospects for the Future* (New York: McGraw-Hill, 1984), p. 229.

5. Ibid.

6. Ibid.

7. Ibid.

8. For the earliest and one of the better critical presentations of this development see Raymond E. Callahan, *Education and the Cult of Efficiency* (Chicago: Univ. of Chicago Press, 1962).

9. Goodlad, *A Placed Called School,* p. 80.

10. Philip W. Jackson, *Life in Classrooms* (New York: Holt, Rinehart and Winston, 1968), pp. 10 and 17.

11. Philip A. Cusick, *Inside High School: The Student's World* (New York: Holt, Rinehart and Winston, 1973), p. 48.

12. Mortimer Adler, *The Paideia Proposal* (New York: Macmillan, 1982).

13. For an extensive discussion of citizen participation see R. Freeman Butts, *The Revival of Civic Learning: A Rationale for Citizenship Education in American Schools* (Phi Delta Kappa Educational Foundation, 1980), chap. 4.

14. On a national level one of the very exciting developments is the growing interest in creating programs for national service. Such a call — "for young men and women" — was included in Malcolm G. Scully's, the "Nation Is Urged to Link College With Civil Goals," *The Chronicle of Higher Education* vol. 21, no. 3(18 Sept. 1985): p. 1.

CHAPTER 3

1. L. Frank Baum, *The Wizard of Oz* (New York: Ballantine Books, 1984).

2. Robert V. Bullough, Jr., Stanley L. Goldstein, and Ladd Holt, *Human Interest in the Curriculum: Teaching and Learning in a Technological Society* (New York: Teachers College Press, 1984), pp. 29–37.

3. Jeannie Oakes, Keeping Track: *How Schools Structure Inequality* (New Haven: Yale Univ. Press, 1985), pp. 48–49.

4. Ibid., pp. 6, 8, 9, and 13.

5. June Cox, Neil Daniel, and Bruce O. Boston, *Educating Able Learners: Programs and Promising Practice* (Austin, Texas: Univ. of Texas Press, 1985).

6. One of the remarkable developments within American education is that at the same time that arguments are being made for separate programs for bright children there is a strong move to mainstream handicapped children in regular classrooms. One wonders why the logic of mainstreaming is not as compelling for bright children as it is for other "special needs" children, including the mildly retarded.

7. Cox, *Educating Able Learners,* p. 127.

8. Ibid., p. 81.

9. Ibid., p. 25.

10. Ibid., p. 154.

11. Robert V. Bullough Jr., "Community Conflict: Gifted Education in Lowell Elementary School" (paper presented at the Annual Bergamo Curriculum Theory Conference, Dayton, Ohio), Oct. 1986.

12. Cox, *Educating Able Learners,* p. 123.

13. Ibid., p. 124–25.

14. Oakes, *Keeping Track,* p. 126.

15. Thomas L. Good and Jere Brophy, *Looking in Classrooms* (New York: Harper and Row, 1984).

16. Oakes, *Keeping Track,* p. 208.

17. Ibid., p. 210.

CHAPTER 4

1. The history of testing is discussed in Leon J. Kamin, *The Science and Politics of I.Q.* (New York: John Wiley and Sons, 1974). See also Stephen J. Gould, *The Mismeasure of Man* (New York: W. W. Norton, 1981).

2. This figure is provided by David Owen in *None of the Above: Behind the Myth of Scholastic Aptitude* (Boston: Houghton Mifflin, 1985), p. 294.

3. See Ibid., pp. 11–13.

4. Walt Haney, "Making Testing More Educational," *Educational Leadership*, 43 (October 1985): p. 6.

5. Reported by The Institute for Research on Teaching, Michigan State University, *Communication Quarterly* 7 (Spring 1985): pp. 1, 4.

6. Allan Nairn, "The Reign of ETS: The Corporation That Makes up Minds," Ralph Nader Report on the Educational Testing Service, 1980, p. 202.

7. Mayo Mohs, "I.Q.," *Discover* vol. 3, no. 9 (September 1982): p. 20.

8. *Deseret News,* (Salt Lake City, Utah) 25 Aug., 1985, sec. B, p.1.

9. Donna Deyhle, "Between Games and Failure: Students and Testing," *Curriculum Inquiry* vol. 13, no. 4 (Winter 1983): p. 372.

10. Owen, *Behind the Myth,* p. 122.

11. David M. White, "Two Views of Standardized Testing," *Harvard Educational Review* vol. 55, no. 3 (August 1985): p. 335.

12. *Ibid.*

13. John W. Gardner, *Excellence* (New York: W. W. Norton, 1984), p. 116.

14. Ibid., pp. 120–21.

CHAPTER 5

1. Theodore Sizer, *Horace's Compromise: The Dilemma of the American High School* (Boston: Houghton Mifflin, 1984), p. 201.

2. Paul Mattingly, *The Classless Profession* (New York: New York Univ. Press, 1975).

3. Linda Darling-Hammond, *Beyond the Commission Reports: The Coming Crisis in Teaching* (Santa Monica, Calif.: The Rand Corp., July 1984), p. 9.

4. Ibid., p. 10.

5. Reported in Judith E. Lanier, *Research on Teacher Education* (E. Lansing, Mich.: Institute for Research on Teaching, September 1984), p. 41.

6. In a recent poll, 63 percent of the public thought higher salaries were the most important way to improve teacher quality. 52 percent said they favored "more funds for public education and teacher training even if it means higher taxes." The level of salary increase supported was between $4,000 and $5,000 so that an elementary school teacher would earn approximately $27,000 and a high school teacher about $29,000. *New York Times,* 2 July 1985, sec. A, p. 13.

It strikes me as odd that we continue to believe the work of the high schools more important than that of the elementary schools as indicated by our willingness to pay high school teachers more.

7. Phillip Jackson, *Life in Classrooms* (New York: Holt, Rinehart and Winston, 1968).

8. *Deseret News,* (Salt Lake City, Utah), 4 December 1985, sec. A, p. 14.

9. *New York Times,* 2 July 1985, sec. A, p. 13.

10. David Owen, *None of the Above: Behind the Myth of Scholastic Aptitude* (Boston: Houghton Mifflin, 1985), chap. 12.

11. Florida Department of Education, *Review of the Florida Performance Measurement System* (Tallahassee, Florida: May 1984), p. 1.

12. Florida Coalition for the Development of a Performance Measurement System: Office of Teacher Education, Certification, and Inservice Staff Development, *Domains: Knowledge Base of the Florida Performance Measurement System* (Tallahassee, Florida, 1983), Foreword.

13. Florida Dept. of Education, *Review,* p. 3.

14. Albert Shanker, "Where We Stand," *New York Times,* 15 Sept. 1985.

15. August Franza, "Facets: The Nation's Response to Criticism of Education: Are We Still 'At Risk?' " *The English Journal* vol. 74, no. 6 (October 1985): p. 22.

16. Darling-Hammond, *Commission Reports,* pp. 13–14.

17. Donna Kerr, "Teaching Competence and Teacher Education in the United States," *Teachers College Record* vol. 84, no. 3 (Spring 1983).

CHAPTER 6

1. Sherry Keith, *Politics of Textbook Selection,* NIE Project Report No. 81–A7, April 1981, p. 1.

2. Ibid., p. 15.

3. People for the American Way, *Attacks On the Freedom to Learn: A 1983–1984 Report,* p.7.

4. Phyllis Schlafy, "Influencing Our Children," *Buffalo Evening News,* 16 Oct. 1981.

5. People for the American Way, *Freedom to Learn,* p. 7.

6. People for the American Way, *As Texas Goes, So Goes the Nation: A Report on Textbook Selection in Texas,* 1983, p. 4.

7. People for the American Way, *Freedom to Learn,* p. 7.

8. Steven Schafersman, *Statement to the Texas State Board of Education to Advocate Abolishing the Board Rules Regulating the Topic of Evolution in Science Textbooks,* Texas Council for Science Education, 12 May 1983, p. 1.

9. People for the American Way, *As Texas Goes,* p. 9.

10. Ibid., p. 8

11. Ibid.

12. Ibid., p. 6.

13. Jean Anyon, "Social Class and the Hidden Curriculum of Work," *The Journal of Education* vol. 162, no. 1 (Winter 1980).

14. Ibid., p. 79.

15. Ibid., p. 81.

16. Ibid., p. 83.

17. Thomas L. Good, "Teacher Effects," *Making Our Schools More Effective: Proceedings of Three State Conferences,* Far West Laboratory for Educational Research and Development, June 1984, pp. 109–132.

18. Ezra Bowen, "The Publishers Flunk Science: California Rejects Textbooks as Skimpy, Especially on Evolution," *Time* 30 Sept. 1985, p. 86.

19. The Holmes Group, *Tomorrow's Teachers: A Report of the Holmes Group* (E. Lansing, Mich: Michigan State Univ., 1986), p. 4.

20. Ibid., p. 5.

21. Ibid., pp. 16–17.

22. See The Carnegie Forum on Education and the Economy, *A Nation Prepared: Teachers for the 21st Century,* The Report of the Task Force on Teaching as a Profession, Carnegie Corp. of New York, May 1986.

23. John I. Goodlad, *A Place Called School: Prospects for the Future* (New York: McGraw-Hill 1984), p. 210.

24. Ibid., p. 211.

25. Ibid.

26. Ibid., p. 212.

27. Ibid.

CHAPTER 7

1. Michael Ende, *The Neverending Story* (New York: Penguin Books, 1984).

2. Ibid., p. 12.

3. Ibid., p. 97.

4. Ibid., p. 115.

5. Ibid., p. 127.

6. Ibid., p. 167.

7. Ibid., p. 172

8. Ibid., p. 255.

9. Ibid., p. 372.

10. Ibid., p. 376.

11. Carnegie Forum on Education and the Economy, *A Nation Prepared: Teachers for the 21st Century,* Report of the Task Force on Teaching as a Profession, Carnegie Corporation of New York, May 1986, p. 20.

12. Vera John-Steiner, *Notebooks of the Mind* (Albuquerque: Univ. of New Mexico Press, 1985), p. 40.

13. Ibid., p. 3.

14. Ibid., p. 79.

15. Ibid., p. 49.

16. Ibid., p. 222.

17. Ibid., pp. 67–68

18. Ibid., p. 180.

19. Ibid., p. 126.

20. Jacob W. Getzels and Philip W. Jackson, *Creativity and Intelligence* (New York: John Wiley and Sons, 1962), pp. 123–132.

21. John-Steiner, *Notebooks of the Mind,* p. 79.

22. Ibid., p. 176.

23. Ibid., p. 36.

24. Ibid., p. 45.

25. John I. Goodlad, *A Place Called School: Prospects for the Future* (New York: McGraw-Hill, 1984), p. 219.

26. Maxine Greene, "Consciousness and the Public Space: Discovering a Pedagogy," *Phenomenology and Pedagogy,* vol. 1, no. 2 (1985) p. 77. This article is rich in important ideas.

27. Marjorie J. Kostelnik, Alice P. Whiren, and Laura C. Stein, in "Living with He-Man: Managing Superhero Fantasy Play," *Young Children* vol. 41, no. 4 (May 1986): pp. 3–9, point out the importance of listening to children's stories. If we listen carefully several themes emerge. One that constantly crops up in my sons' stories is a need to have a measure of power and control over their lives. They imagine they have power even when they do not. Simultaneously, they explore ways of achieving it, sometimes through superheroes, but other times through building planes or snow fortresses impervious to the attacks of enemies.

28. One of the prominent themes in John-Steiner's book is the importance of childhood as a source of creativity.

29. Goodlad, *A Place Called School,* p. 220.

CHAPTER 8

1. Israel Scheffler, *The Language of Education* (Springfield, Ill.: Charles C. Thomas, 1960), p. 48.

2. Ibid., p. 49.

3. While working on this chapter, I came across an article by Phillip C. Schlechty and Anne Walker Joslin, "Images of Schools," *Teachers College Record* vol. 86, no. 1 (Fall 1984): pp. 156–70, from which I borrowed the "log" metaphor.

4. Robert N. Bellah et al., *Habits of the Heart: Individualism and Commitment in American Life* (Berkeley: Univ. of California Press, 1985), pp. 8, 290.

5. Ibid., p. 163.

6. Ibid., p. 282.

7. Fred M. Newman and Donald W. Oliver, "Education and Community," in *Curriculum and the Cultural Revolution,* ed. David E. Purpel and Maurice Belanger (Berkeley, Calif.: McCutchan Publishing Corp., 1972), pp. 207–8.

8. *Ibid.,* p. 209.

INDEX

Adler, Mortimer, 31, 34, 105
Advanced placement courses, 42,
    87–88
Arts and creativity, 119–20

Baldwin, James, 116, 118
Baum, L. Frank, 37
Bennett, William, 7, 9
*Brown vs. Topeka Board of
    Education,* 99
Burns, Robert, 64
Butts, R. Freeman, 19–20

Carnegie Forum, 103, 112–13
Carnegie Foundation for the
    Advancement of Teaching, 24
Cartier-Bresson, Henri, 119
Citizenship, 9, 17, 131; as
    educational aim, 7, 10, 14, 20;
    obligations of, 4
Community: conflict and conflict
    avoidance, 134–35; creation of,
    131; defined, 129–30; and
    education, 130–31; and public
    schooling, 132–36
Competition, 12, 30; and school
    reform, 7, 9
Consumption, conspicuous, 17
Cooperative learning, 47
Creativity: and the arts, 119–20;
    cultivation of, 115–22; dulling

of, 112, 115, 122; qualities of
    mind, 116–17

Decision making, centralization of,
    17
Democracy, 9; and excellence, 64
Democratic traditions, 19
Double Helix, The, 95

Education, higher: 18, 100–104
Educational Testing Service, 52, 55
Einstein, Albert, 64, 117
Evaluation, teacher: 77–79

Finn, Chester, 7
Freedom, 9; as a condition for the
    development of creativity, 118
Fromm, Erich, 82

Gabler, Mel and Norma, on
    citizenship, 93
Gardner, John, 63
Getzels, Jacob, 117–18
Gifted, education of, 42–44
Goodlad, John, 26, 31
Grouping, homogenous: 43, 44

Hatch, Orrin, 7, 9

Honig, Bill, 100
Horace's Compromise, 68

Individual development, as part of
    community, 21
Individual differences, 40
Individualism, 19, 129, 130
Instruction: as coaching, 32, 33, 34;
    as lecturing, 32; as Socratic
    dialogue, 32, 33, 34
Interests: common, 8, 125, 132, 134;
    and community, 130–31; special,
    125, 132

Jackson, Philip, 117, 118
Jefferson, Thomas, 8, 12; and the
    Bill for the More General
    Diffusion of Knowledge, 4, 7–8;
    on false and natural aristocracy,
    8; on the public world, 8–9
John-Steiner, Vera, 115–18

Kerr, Donna, 86
Knowledge: as power, 99–100; as
    symbolic capital, 100

Labelling, 38–49, 135; as means of
    justifying school failure, 48
Labor: degradation of, 131;
    deskilling of, 16
Learning communities, 88–89
Lecturing, 32
Lieberman, Myron, 7

Mann, Horace, 4, 9, 16, 71
Media, mass: 17–18
Merit, 121; and testing, 52; and
    virtue, 15
Metaphors, school: community, 129–
    36; factory, 123–24, 126, 128–
    29, 132–33; family, 125, 132;
    information network, 128; log,

127; marketplace, 123–25, 132;
    marathon, 127; social event and
    necessary evil, 125–26; war
    zone, 126; zoo, 126

Needs, 15–16, 25, 38, 40; assignment
    of, 45–46
Neverending Story, The, 109–12

Politics, 9
Public world: as arena for competing
    interests, 9; classical ideal of, 9;
    deflation of, 21; disengagement
    from, 17; enhancement of, 35,
    136; and excellence, 64–66; and
    school content, 99; values of, 19

Schlafly, Phyllis, 92
School: as community, 20, 132–36;
    as disconnected from the public
    world, 34. *See also* Public world
School, content of: different for
    different kinds of students, 96–
    98; responsibility of higher
    education, 100–104; and the
    survey course, 98
Schooling, private, 6, 10; and
    vouchers, 5–6
Schooling, public: and creativity,
    112–15; curriculum of, 5, 91–
    108; defense of, 10–16;
    economistic views of, 133; and
    excellence, 50–66; expectations
    of, viii, ix, 5, 6; and the factory
    model, 30, 52; and graduation
    standards, 12; importance of, 3,
    4; and individual competition,
    12, 13; and justice, 13; and
    justification of failure, 13; loss
    of faith in, 3, 10; and merit, 12,
    113; and occupational structure,
    15, 16; and the public world, 16;
    purposes of, 7, 10, 12, 14, 15,
    16, 19–20, 30, 99; and sorting,

13–14, 30; and standardization, 31; tracking within, 5, 13, 40; and vouchers, 6. *See also* Metaphors, school; Public world; Sorting; Tracking

School reform: and competition, 7; and imagination, 123; and labelling, 48; and marketplace values, 7; need for new language, 49; and the public world, 18, 136; and social relationships, 126; and the teacher role, 86–89; and teachers, 70; test score, excellence as aim of, 50

Social studies, 105–8

Socratic dialogue, 32

Sorting, 13, 38–49; categories used, 39; institutionalization of categories, 39; and testing, 52. *See also* Tracking

Students: good students described, 23; images of, 124–28; and passivity, 27, 28, 31; role of, 24, 25, 69–70; and schooling, 24, 26–27; and self-interest, 24

Teacher associations, 76–77

Teacher education, 101–3

Teachers: accountability pressures on, 75; and autonomy, 83; and burnout, 48; images of, 124–28; isolation of, 33, 80, 82–83; lack of control over professional lives, 76; low status of, 70–73;

professionalism, 87, 88; qualities and skills of, 32–33, 70; and rapid workpace, 74; the "real world" of, 69–89; roles of, 69–70; survival strategies of, 82–85

Teaching: and bureaucracy and hierarchy, 76; and career ladders, 75; as coaching, 31; contradictory nature of, 79–80; feminization of, 71; standardization of, 77; as telling, 27–28, 32

Testing, standardized: 51–66; assumptions about, 53–60; critical discourse about, 65–66; cultural and social class bias in, 57–58; fascination with, 51; student preparation for, 54, 55–56; test taking as a skill, 62–63; validity of, 53–57

Textbooks, 91; adoption of, 92–94; censorship of, 92–95; market influences on, 92

Tracking: assumptions of, 40–47; effects of, 43, 44–45, 46, 97, 135; and misplacement, 45. *See also* Grouping; Sorting

Vocation, as an educational aim, 10–12, 20

Vocationalism, 24

Vouchers, 6, 9, 15

Work, 16–17